COMING WEST

A Natural History of Home

COMING WEST

A Natural History of Home

Kevin Van Tighem

preface by Peter Christensen
drawings by Stephen Hutchings

Altitude Publishing
The Canadian Rockies/Vancouver

Publication Information

Altitude Publishing Canada Ltd.

1500 Railway Avenue
Canmore, Alberta T1W 1P6

Copyright © 1997, Altitude Publishing Canada Ltd.
Copyright © text 1997, Kevin Van Tighem
Copyright © preface 1997, Peter Christensen
Copyright © drawings 1997, Stephen Hutchings

Canadian Cataloguing in Publication Data

Van Tighem, Kevin J., 1952 -
Coming West

ISBN 1-55153-911-X
1. Natural History – Canada, Western. 2. Canada, Western – Description and travel. I. Title.
QH106.2W4V36 1997   508.712   C97-910745-8

Made in Western Canada

Printed and bound in Canada
by Friesen Printers, Altona, Manitoba.

Altitude GreenTree Program

Altitude will plant in Canada twice as many trees
as were used in the manufacturing of this product.

Project Development

Art direction	Stephen Hutchings
Drawings	Stephen Hutchings
Design	Kelly Stauffer
Project management	Sharon Komori
Layout	Sabrina Grobler
	& Kelly Stauffer
Style editing	Sabrina Grobler
Substantive editing	Peter Christensen
Financial management	Laurie Smith
Sales management	Scott Davidson

Contents

Acknowledgements

MY HEARTFELT APPRECIATION to my wife, Gail, and to Corey, Katie and Brian, for their support, patience and love through all the times when I have been writing instead of doing things with them.

Red Wilkinson, for many years the editor and publisher of *Western Sportsman* magazine, was the first editor to offer me advice and encouragement as a writer. Over the years, his magazine published many of my articles, including "Medicine Trout" and "Forgotten Rainbows."

David Dodge single-handedly produced *Borealis,* for a few short years one of the finest environmental magazines in Canada, on a computer in his basement. "Curse of the Cow"; "Clogged Arteries"; and "Posterity will Bless Us" originally appeared in *Borealis.*

Lynn Zwicky was editor of *Environment Views* before and after it ceased to be an arm's-length publication of *Alberta Environment.* Like too many of the Alberta government's hasty privatizations, the end result was that Albertans lost a great magazine. Articles that originally appeared in *Environment Views* are: "Bow Corridor: Heart of a Mountain Ecosystem"; "Through a Grizzly's Eyes: Ecosystem thinking in a fragmented world"; "Unicorns in the Whaleback"; and "Save the Gopher!"

"Olden Days Creek"; "Environmental Education"; "Witnesses in the Wild"; "In Praise of Cows"; "Irrigation, Habitat and Hope"; "A Plague of Roads"; and "Quality" first appeared in *The Outdoor Edge.*

"Grandfather's Trout"; "The Tree and the Trout"; "Who Speaks for Running Waters?"; and "Of Wave Pools and Stream 'Enhancement'" were first published in *Trout Canada.*

Park News printed "Have Our National Parks Failed

Us?"; *Nature Canada* published "Gray Ghosts." *Flyfishing* published "The Flower of Fishes." "Memories on the Water" first appeared in *BowBenders Hunting Annual*. "Better Anthropocentrism" appeared in *The Trumpeter*. "Violence at Mountain Park" was a guest editorial for the *Jasper Booster* and the *Hinton Parklander*.

"Whoopers," the only short story in this book, was printed in *Event*, a literary journal published by Douglas College in B.C. It was later reprinted in the 1989 *Journey Prize Anthology* by McClelland and Stewart, and another anthology: *Dutch Voices*.

This book is dedicated to the memory of the late Ian D. Jack, conservationist, mentor, and friend. He saved the Columbia River wetlands.

Kevin Van Tighem, Waterton, AB
June, 1997

Preface

PASSIONATE, REASONABLE, humorous, self-effacing, stubborn and insightful are just a few of the adjectives that come to mind in describing Kevin Van Tighem's *Coming West*. These vibrant stories and personal essays are forged of knowledge, understanding and experience. This is no polemic but solid work crafted out of an uninhibited and guileless love of the land. There is no greater complexity than our constantly changing relationship with the world, with each other and with nature. It is with no less a subject that Kevin Van Tighem is entangled.

I met Kevin twenty-five years ago when he worked as a seasonal Park Naturalist at Kootenay Park. Our need to write and to talk about writing is what brought us together then. Our communication over the years has been sporadic but I have always taken a keen interest in his many articles in outdoor magazines. You see, Kevin walks the fine line between the hunters and the anti-hunters, between ideology and current reality. That is what makes him different and interesting. You will not find him demonizing his opponents or their cause, nor will you find him serving up platitudes and emotion as truth.

What you will encounter when you read Kevin's finely tuned essays and stories is a keen truth-seeker deeply in love with the land.

Shortly after I met Kevin, I heard that he was in the hospital following a bird watching expedition in southwestern Alberta. I wondered in amazement how one can get hurt bird watching. Had he overturned his canoe? Did he miss while chopping firewood? I phoned Dale, a mutual friend, to find out what had happened and how badly hurt he was.

Kevin had camped at Cowley, Alberta, near the Castle River. A group of hardened party animals intent on getting it on moved into a nearby site. As the night progressed, despite repeated and increasingly less polite requests to shut down the mind-thumping adolescent mating call of amplified stereo speakers, the party became progressively louder.

Finally, as dawn began to break, the young Van Tighem lost it. He erupted from his tent, exchanged a few hostile words with his alcohol-steeped neighbors, and then aimed an unerring blow with his axe at the offending stereo speaker. For a moment, the predawn peace returned. Robins sang tentatively. Owls hooted. But the astonished and offended partiers were not amused. They meted a quick and violent revenge, and this was why my friend was in the hospital.

It seems that bird watching can be a dangerous sport after all.

Kevin would be fine in a week or two. Superficial wounds. But what we now knew, aside from the fact that he would recover, was that this was someone who would stand up for what he believed in. This story reminded me of V.S. Naipal's realization concerning justice in his book *Finding the Centre*: "...I had arrived at the conviction — the conviction that is at the root of so much human anguish and passion, and corrupts so many lives — that there is justice in the world."

For several years Kevin was a regular columnist for *The Outside Edge*, a magazine that targets hunters and fishers in the western provinces. In his column, "The Land Ethic," he wrote an article arguing that setting out bait for bear hunting was unethical and unsportsmanlike. Another regular columnist wrote an article defending the practice. After publishing both points of view, the editor — for vaguely stated reasons — decided to drop Kevin's column. I have long admired Kevin's courage to walk among the lions and to tackle difficult issues. Unfortunately — and, I believe, to the detriment of the hunting and fishing community — the editors of *The Outside Edge* chose to run off the cliff rather than walk the line by continuing to let opposing points of view have their say. Kevin's regular column now appears in *The Alberta Game Warden*.

We live in a confusing time. All the information we have available has not made our choices about land use easier. How do we sort out the daunting questions about humanity's relationship with itself and nature? Just what do these choices, once made, mean when we humans put the rubber to the road? Are there solutions? Do our values match our actions?

To whom can we turn for answers to these difficult questions? Or maybe that is not quite right. Where can we turn for informed opinion and truthful discussion? The Captains of media spin? The international eco-purist? The well-fed academics in their ivory towers? I have heard copious diatribes from the self-appointed eco-pundits and yet I do not feel well equipped to choose a direction.

This is where writers like Van Tighem, Lopez, Waters, Rowe, Murphy, Gayton or Hasselstrom fit in. As surely as the cattail with a red winged blackbird perched on its tip is grown out of a prairie slough, so the informed and authentic voice of Van Tighem was born of his experiences on the land and the consideration thereof.

The clear voice we hear singing in *Coming West: A Natural History of Home* is that of Kevin Van Tighem of the western plains and mountain country — striving to understand, striving to do the right thing, and striving to pass on to his listeners a depth of understanding which can and does make sense of complex issues. Through story telling and personal realization, Van Tighem makes a statement that is unquestionably for the land, and for its people.

Peter Christensen, Radium Hot Springs, B.C.
May, 1997

Introduction

Introduction

MANY OF THESE ESSAYS have been published previously. I offer them as an edited collection because I believe they say more together than apart.

Here are environmental essays, hunting stories, nature interpretation, philosophical rants and fishing tales. It may seem, on first impression, to be an odd assemblage. Surely I should come down clearly on one side of some fence or other. I can only say that, to me, fences have always seemed to deny the reality of landscape. Some build and tend to fences; others find more value in trying to understand the underlying landscape.

In assembling writings, some of which date back to the mid-1980s, I had to resolve the question of whether to update them in light of subsequent history. In the end, for the most part, I chose to tinker as little as possible. Instead, I noted the year in which the original was first published. Dams proposed have become dams built. The pulp mill expansions of the late 1980s in northern Alberta are history; roads and clearcuts continue to spread. Sometimes, my own perspective on the issues has changed — as, for example, with "The Curse of the Cow." Letting the older writings speak out of their own time seemed more fair, however, than to try to adapt them to a later time and a later voice.

I asked Peter Christensen, a friend who lives in the shadow of B.C.'s Brisco Range, to edit this collection. Peter challenged weaknesses in my logic and tried to head me off whenever I began to polemicize or accuse. If any preachiness or nagging survives, it is in spite of Peter's advice.

These are challenging times for those who value the wild. The population of my home province, Alberta, has more than quadrupled in my short lifetime. Generations of western-ers have grown up expecting to find jobs where and when we want them and to enjoy a high material quality of life. Simultaneously, we have expected to live in a clean environ-ment with abundant wildlife and freedom to wander at will in natural settings. We have spent more than a century rearrang-ing the West to meet our needs and expectations, and fighting over the consequences. We all live in this place, but we do not like what seems to be happening here. Unintended conse-quences are the norm, not the exception.

I think that the growing polarization, paranoia and hopelessness that permeate so much of the debate over environ-mental issues are fueled by a profound — and widespread — lack of environmental literacy. This lack is as evident when some people describe the natural environment as "delicate" or "balanced" as when others dismiss the concerns of environmen-talists as emotional or dishonest. Biologists, industry consul-tants, environmental groups, hunters and anglers all profess far more insight than any can honestly claim to have. Little won-der that increasingly we face the future with uncertainty, and each other with distrust.

I thought of putting this book off until I had solutions to propose. Real solutions, however, may be more elusive than the twentieth-century plague of experts would like us to believe. The best we may hope to achieve is to understand more, and try harder. We must never cease trying to learn how to live as if we are a part of the living West — not apart from it. I believe we can only do so if we strive — with all the curiosity, intelligence, passion and humour of which humans are capable — to understand better the living ecosystems most of us pro-fess to love so well.

If we cannot begin to understand the places where we live, how can we profess to live there? Are we at home in the West, or are we merely an army of occupation? What must we learn to see, so that we can find our way home? These questions underlie this book's explorations into the endlessly complex and wonderfully real world of western Canada. There may be no clear answer to the question of how to live lives that are worthy of this place. Still, we must never stop asking.

And there is every reason to delight in the sheer glory of the quest.

An Angler's West

Olden Days Creek

DAD USED TO TELL ME about the olden days, when he and my Grandfather fished remote streams in the far, lonely valleys of the Rocky Mountains. His tales were tinged with regret that the kind of fishing they had enjoyed in those days was long gone. By the time I got my first fishing rod, new roads penetrated into the back of beyond. Anglers were everywhere. I grew up nostalgic for days I had never known, regretting the fate that waited to place me on this Earth until other people's boots had tracked up every stream bank.

In the olden days one could be alone on trout streams where the water was as pure as the air, and cold as ice. The valleys were wild and seldom visited by humans. Streams teemed with trout. They were easy to catch. There were moose in the meadows and the possibility of a grizzly around every bend. In the olden days, a determined angler could still find pools had no other fisherman had ever seen.

I pored over Dad's maps in a forlorn search for lonely creeks that other anglers, by some miracle, might have overlooked. I insisted to Dad that there still must be some olden day creeks left out there somewhere. We certainly checked out all the possibilities. It was a search that enriched my boyhood summers. Still, by the time I grew up and left home I had come to believe that fishing for undisturbed populations of native trout had become the stuff of legend.

Even so, I never quite surrendered the belief that somewhere, temporarily forgotten, there must yet be one or two little bits of yesterday. Faith, Mom used to tell me, eventually will be rewarded.... One summer, I decided to follow up on a fishing story I had heard a decade earlier. Map in hand, I drove down a woods road far from the highway. At length I pulled off

21

and parked where the map showed a small meadow stream — the headwaters of a well-known river — not too far off the road. There was no sign of running water anywhere; just lodge-pole pines and heat haze. Stepping out into an eager swarm of hungry mosquitoes, I donned waders and vest and set off into the resin-scented shade of the forest.

Sunbeams pierced the forest canopy and dappled the forest floor. It was late morning. Few birds sang, but some-where ahead I could hear the plaintive, "Quick! Three beers!" cry of an olive-sided flycatcher: beaver pond music. I was in the right place.

After a few hundred yards of forest-shadow and dead-fall, I emerged into a long, narrow meadow of sedge and reed-grass. Halfway across the meadow a meandering line of willows marked the course of Olden Days Creek.

Several trout darted away downstream as I stepped to the edge of the stream. The creek was clear and sleek, eddying against the willow tangles and feeling its way into the sedge marsh and out again. A submerged jungle of sedge, undulating gently, stretched out in the direction of the current.

The fleeing trout vanished into the watery tangle, and the stream was suddenly empty, winking innocently in the sun-shine.

I stepped back from the edge. Hands already shaking from excitement, I tied on a bucktail caddis. On the first cast several trout appeared magically and raced each other for my fly. So began one of the finest days fishing in my life.

The creek was full of native west-slope cutthroat trout, deep-bodied and richly patterned with orange and salmon markings. Most were in the six to ten inch range. I soon found that my biggest challenge today would be keeping the eager lit-tle fellows off the hook long enough to allow the bigger trout to bite. The big ones were only twelve to fifteen inches long but in a stream barely five feet wide, catching one was like hooking a beaver. I caught many.

That was the first of several visits to a stream time seems to have forgotten. I have yet to see another angler there.

Olden Days Creek, I learned during my long hours of trying to learn its secrets, is more stable than many other mountain streams. It flows at the bottom of a long, wide valley. In late June its meadows are marsh, with treacherous little beaver runs waiting to submerge the unwary angler. The marshy valley floor absorbs the spring runoff, protecting the stream channel from high flows that might otherwise damage it.

Later in the summer, springs seep from the banks along the valley, maintaining the stream's flow by discharging water trapped by the porous forest soils. From creekside, all that is visible is green meadow, old-growth spruce and pine, and the tops of the surrounding mountains. I knew that loggers had been busy in some parts of the valley, but Olden Days Creek, so far, showed no sign of having noticed them.

One evening I picked up the kids after work and we headed out to explore the headwaters of Olden Days Creek more thoroughly. The stream winds through beaver ponds and marshes and loses itself in a deep lake before fanning through a vast plain of waving reeds. A mile farther its channel emerges again, meandering through more sedge meadows and willow. On foot, quagmire and marsh had turned me back time and again. This time we had the canoe on the roof of the van.

I carried the canoe down the forested slope to the water-meadow, two little life-jacketed figures bobbing along behind me. Leaving them seated beside each other on the canoe, I went back for paddles and gear. A snipe winnowed above the meadow. A moose stood stock-still a few hundred yards upstream, watching as I loaded the kids into the canoe.

23

We launched the canoe beside an ancient beaver dam overgrown with swamp birch and willows. The kids chattered excitedly, then became silent as the canoe approached the spot where the water pours over the dam into a fast little chute.

"I don't want to go over that waterfall, Daddy," said Katie, the four-year-old.

"Hang on," I replied.

The canoe teetered on the brink of the chute, then tilted and slid into the tailrace. I steered us into a long bay where the creek widened and shallowed, then lost itself into the dark water of a small lake.

Something laughed.

"What's that?" said Corey.

"A loon."

The loon watched us impassively as we skimmed the marly shallows. Pondweeds gave way to inky black where the bottom dropped suddenly away.

"It's deep," said Katie, mournfully. She sat very stiff and straight, a little hand clenching each gunwale.

The loon disappeared. The kids watched for it to surface again. I tied on a scud pattern and fed line out over the edge. The loon played peekaboo with us as we trolled the drop off.

The valley turned gold as the sun dropped lower in the sky. At length I conceded that this was not the day I would prove my theory about this lake holding big trout. I brought in the line and set us on a course for the lake outlet, another shallow, marl-bottomed bay.

"Look for leeches," I said.

"What are they?"

"Black wormy things that suck your blood if you fall in."

"I don't like this place," Katie muttered.

24

"There's one!" shouted Corey.

Katie said, very softly, "Yuck."

We drifted quietly along. The kids leaned over the gunwales and watched the leeches and water bugs. Schools of minnows squirted off to the side or hung suspended like silver slivers in the crystal water. Ahead, tall jointed stems of water rushes formed a jungle wall where the stream widened and disappeared into a wide marsh.

Out of the corner of my eye I saw movement. For a moment my heart nearly stopped; it looked like the biggest fish I had ever seen. Then I realized I was looking at a beaver swimming underwater, parallel to us. I pointed him out to the kids.

The beaver's big feet kicked up puffs of marl with each stroke. His eyes were clearly visible as we veered closer to him; he twisted his body and went burrowing away from us into the reeds.

"Look," I said, "You can see where he is. The reeds are waving."

Waving, clattering reeds marked the beaver's course, like a slow wind twisting its way through the marsh.

Then we slipped into the marsh ourselves. The reeds closed around the canoe. The channel vanished. The only clues to the direction of flow were grasses and leaves all strung out in one direction and the movement of bits of debris along the bottom. It was too shallow to paddle so I used the paddles to pole the canoe through the rattling reeds.

At length, open water appeared ahead. We emerged into an open pond that lay along an old beaver dam. Water poured through a gap.

Landing, I lifted the kids out one by one, then pulled the canoe up on the dam. We stretched the stiffness out of our legs and looked around. As far as the eye could see there were only marsh, forest, and mountains — all lit with the rich, golden glow of a Rocky Mountain sunset. No jet trails, no roads, no sound except the whine of mosquitoes and the singing of Lincoln's sparrows and yellowthroats.

For a moment I stood still, caught by an unexpected sensation of timelessness. Nothing so much as hinted that this was the late twentieth century, or that we were not the first people to visit this place. I half expected to see my grandfather's salt and pepper cap showing above the willows. Looking around, however, all I saw was two small faces looking up impatiently at their bemused father.

I got the kids comfortable on the grass, and then crept over to within casting distance of the outlet. Spilling through the gap in the old dam, the stream roared straight into a willow tangle, eddying out into another long meandering reach.

On my first cast three trout flashed at the fly and one connected. As my rod tip began to dance there came a chorus of shouts: "Did you get one, Dad?"

"He's got a fish."

"I wanna see! I wanna see!"

I tried to hustle the trout out of the pool so it wouldn't disturb the others. It was stubborn, churning up the surface and diving deep into the undercut hole. Finally I got him up on the grass: a fat thirteen inch cutthroat. I need not have worried about disturbing the pool; my next cast brought me a nine-incher that I released into the upstream pond. The next few casts brought fish swirling out of the depths, but it was a while before I hooked another. This one was a fourteen-inch beauty, and completed my limit.

We launched again and went boiling down through the pool into the lower stream. A few hundred yards further, the creek spread out into another reed marsh even more extensive than the first, so I turned the canoe around. We headed back.

The shadows were deep and the evening grown chilly

by the time we reached our original launch site. I stashed the canoe in the woods and ushered the kids up through the forest gloom.

Much later, we arrived home. The kids were full of stories for their Mom. It was well past their usual bedtime before we could get them to sleep.

Later, I phoned Dad to tell him about our evening. I could have waited until our next visit, I suppose. But he and I had spent many days afield hunting for Olden Days Creek. I wanted to tell him that the kids and I had just been there, and it was every bit as good as the olden days he had described. Maybe even better. ✤ *(1990)*

Grandfather's Trout

I WAS BORN IN 1952. That same year, the gates closed on the St. Mary's River Dam in southern Alberta, dooming another migratory bull trout stock to extinction. Even if people had known then what we now know about the destruction caused by on-stream dams, it's unlikely anybody would have cared all that much. In the 1950s bull trout were easy protein at best, and junk fish at worst. Anglers of the day commonly tossed them up into the bushes to rot — just as they did with suckers — to reduce the competition for "real" trout.

My life has seen the construction of the Dickson Dam on the Red Deer, the Paddle River Dam, and the Three Rivers Dam on the Oldman. Each dam forever impaired whole river ecosystems and cut native stocks of bull trout off from their headwaters spawning grounds. The last fish died of old age without replacement. Only their ghosts now hunt whitefish in the eddies and log jams of the tamed, degraded rivers.

Many of us fought long and hard to save one or more of those rivers. The people who built those dams were arrogant, narrow-minded technocrats — ah, we knew them well. Such wonderful, unseen enemies!

It's good to have enemies. It makes life simple when you can paint conservation issues in simple black and white. Increasingly, now, I suspect that some of those devils incarnate I once spent so much time vilifying and fighting against are probably decent human beings. Most, no doubt, have at least as much integrity and public-mindedness as the conservationists who stand opposed to them. I have also come to realize that we can trace the bull trout's biggest problems a lot closer to home than some of us would care to admit.

I grew up in Calgary, a small city at the edge of the Alberta foothills. Although the Bow River was only four blocks away, Dad took us west or north into the headwaters country when it was time to go fishing. This was where Dad had learned to fish a decade or so earlier under the tutelage of his father-in-law: my mother's dad, Alban McParland.

My grandfather was a dedicated fisherman and hunter. I have always regretted that by the time I began fishing he had grown too old to go afield. Although I never got to fish with him, he figures strongly in my memories of fishing and the far places that came to mean so much to me over the years.

Although he had lived most of his life in Alberta, my grandfather was as Irish as they come: a colourful personality and a great storyteller. I remember, as vividly as if it were just yesterday, Pop-Pop's stories about catching big bull trout — there were no small bull trout in his stories — on ruby-eyed wobblers, live mice and raw meat. In the corner of his eyes were lines from having spent so much time out in the wind and the sun. He would sit at the kitchen table, drinking tea and smoking cigarettes while he visited with his only daughter. I watched the scrolling lines of cigarette smoke tracing the sunbeams. The sounds of city traffic outside faded as my grandfather's rough Irish voice carried me away to wild places where huge bull trout cruised the bottoms of canyon pools and grizzlies stalked the timber at night. I never got to know the headwaters country objectively, because I already knew it as a place that resonated out of his stories.

As I grew older, Dad took me with him during Saturday fishing trips and summer camping expeditions into remote country I had never seen before, but had already grown to love. And what country it was: the braided floodplain of the upper Elbow River spilling across the feet of the Rocky Mountain front ranges — the hidden green valleys of Prairie, Meadow and Elk Creeks — the dark forests and long evenings along Shunda Creek and the Burnt Timber. What a glorious land to be young in!

We even went fishing in winter, driving far up the Elbow River and fishing open waters of the mainstem and back channels along its braided floodplain. Dad sometimes caught native cutthroats, but as often as not it was little bull trout that we took home to eat.

My favourite hole was in a small side channel of the Elbow. It was a deep, scoured-out pool beneath a tangled pile of drift logs. Down at the bottom, beneath the logs, I could almost always find a small school of bull trout. They hugged the gravel, white-edged fins barely moving in the near-freezing water of late winter. I would try to tease those silvery-gray fish into biting by jigging my red-and-white spoon up and down in front of their mouths. When that did not work, I tried to snag them. I never got one, nor did I manage to persuade Dad to follow me up from the big pools he fished and try his hand at

29

catching them. I had no idea what kind of fish these were, but their pale grey bodies and bottom-hugging habit told me they probably weren't real trout.

Real trout, of course, were the brookies, rainbows and browns we preferred to catch. Elk Creek, a tributary of the Clearwater, was loaded with brookies and browns when we discovered it. One trip I caught three bull trout, all of them fourteen inches in length. Those were big fish to me, and of course we killed and ate them; I did not know at the time that they were probably not even big enough to be sexually mature. In any case, I made sure they never got a chance to reproduce.

Those big bull trout of my grandfather's stories eluded us, but they always remained a tantalizing possibility. His grand-kids often hiked for hours to get far from the nearest road, peering into new pools and searching for the kind of place that would hold a trout big enough to dine on live mice. Eventually I began to suspect that my grandfather had exaggerated a bit. Surely, after so many long days afield, we would have found at least one or two of those big monsters with which he had so liberally salted his stories.

I realize now that his stories were true. Those big bull trout used to be there — but my grandfather's generation did away with them. My mom gave me a couple of old pictures recently; one shows my grandfather and a friend with thirty-eight huge bull trout strung along a line stretched between two trees at Lower Kananaskis Lake. I guess it never occurred to those fortunate enough to fish the frontier that the big fish could ever run out.

The bull trout we found were small but no less eager to bite a hook than the monsters of my grandfather's day. They were ridiculously easy to catch compared with other trout, sometimes fighting free of the hook only to bite again on the very next cast.

We used to visit one headwater creek where young bull trout were stranded upstream from a reach where the water went into the alluvium. By midsummer, the wakes of startled bull trout disturbed the shrunken pools, but the desperate fish were still willing to chase a spinner. We never had any trouble filling a creel. I haven't been back for years. I hope there are still bull trout in that creek. If there are not, I can take personal credit for helping to wipe out that stock.

It was years later, after I had become an outdoor writer that I began to consider the importance, and potency, of words. So simple and straightforward a term as "trout," like other stereotypes, disguises more than it reveals. I interviewed fisheries biologist Carl Hunt about bull trout one day in his Edson office. He pointed out that bull trout are as different from other trout as they are from catfish or suckers.

Based on that interview and other research, I wrote a magazine article and called it "Frontier Trout." It was a combination of public education and personal expungement of accreted layers of guilt. Dad and I talked several times about the creels full of dried up little bull trout we had poured into the kitchen sink after trips into the back of beyond. We had always considered ourselves conservationists, never taking more than our limit. Now, with the wisdom of hindsight, we could see the degree to which our family, in celebrating the richness of our natural heritage, had helped to deplete it.

My grandfather is dead. So, too, is my dad. Funny how it goes: I have become one of my family's elders even though, in my mind, I'm still the kid who climbed out on those backwater log jams and peered down through the cracks at wintering bull trout. I wish I could remember more of the stories my grandfather told me, because they are like all heritage — once lost, it's almost impossible to retrieve. If I have become an elder, then I suppose I have a responsibility as custodian of the stories that are my family's heritage. But most of them are gone, along with the people who lived them.

Each of us, I have come to realize, is a custodian of our collective heritage — of that part that we have not squandered or lost forever, or that we can yet restore.

Grandfather's trout are part of that shared heritage, and they survive still in some of the streams Dad first showed me. When I go back to the upper Elbow River, Clearwater River or Burnt Timber Creek, I am with Dad again. My grandfather's ghost is there too — just upstream, going around the bend to the next good hole. The chatter of the water sounds the same as it did back then, before all the changes and all the losses. The bull trout are still there.

Who are we, if not the sum of all the places and things and experiences that accrete around our personalities over the years we spend on this earth? My father is still here. My grand-father is here, too — because those streams and bull trout and experiences are still here. I know where to go when I need time alone with my grandfather and father.

Those are other people's boot tracks on the gravel bars of course, and those other anglers have different values, differ-ent experiences, and different knowledge. In some ways, we have come a long way from the 60s and 70s when we all ganged up, unknowingly, to put the skids on the bull trout. In other ways, we have left some important values behind in our haste to escape the past. For my elders, fishing was part of a way of living based on freedom, wild places and rugged inde-pendence, not a form of entertainment.

Still, those modern anglers release the bull trout they catch. Increasingly, they are coming to see the bull trout for what it is: a unique creature adapted to western waters in ways that no exotic trout could ever be. I may feel a twinge of irrita-tion upon seeing their boot tracks beside streams I think of as my own but those are — for the most part — conservationists' boot tracks.

That is one reason grandfather's trout are still out there. And as long as they are, no matter how much we may have forgotten of the details of our common heritage, there will still be opportunities for my children, your children, and children yet unborn. They will still be able to go out to where the wind breathes in the pine trees, newborn waters gossip over the gravel, and elk watch nervously from the sidehills — and to catch and hold a fish that is the distillation of all these things, and more.

The bull trout, the streams where it lives, and the unique western ecosystems that encompass those streams, are my grandfather, and my father, and me. As long as they live on, we all do. Our heritage builds and deepens. We continue, whole. ॐ *(1995)*

Forgotten Rainbows

NOT FAR FROM WHERE I live a small stream slips out of the forest, bubbles unnoticed through a culvert, and slides back into the shadows of an ancient spruce forest. Dozens of vehicles cross it each day. Few, if any, of the drivers even notice the furtive flicker of water beneath alder foliage.

It is not much of a creek. At the widest, it is still narrow enough to jump over. There's little risk of an unwary fisherman going in over the tops of his hip waders. In fact, there's no reason most fishermen would even give it a second look. There are plenty of rivers and lakes in the area that produce big fish.

All the same, I drop in for a visit now and then. I bring

a dozen muddler minnows because I know I am going to leave a few stuck in the alders and spruce overhanging the stream. I flatten the barbs on the hooks with a pair of needle-nosed pliers because I know that I will be releasing quite a few trout. Then I crouch over and force my way into the underbrush to spend a few hours with Alberta's only native rainbow trout.

These rainbows are beautifully marked and scrappy, but never big. It is not trophy fishing, by any means, but it is special. And in catching the little forest trout, I am continuing an angling tradition that goes back almost a century and a half.

On June 14, 1863, Dr. Walter Cheadle wandered away from his party's camp somewhere near where Edson is now. He "...soon captured a small trout of some 2 oz. but could not get another run; the fish was very like an English burn trout, but instead of red spots, it had a red line along each side about 1/8 inch broad; the black spots similar to English variety...."

Fisheries agencies have since introduced Cheadle's English burn trout — which we know as the brown trout — to most parts of western North America. It is now one of the most sought-after fish in the West. The little rainbows, however, live out their lives in muskeg streams and foothills riffles, ignored by all except a few local anglers who like the way the little guys taste when fried up with salt and pepper.

There's a sad irony in the fact that the native Athabasca rainbow trout is both unique and threatened, but receives only neglect. Meanwhile, fishermen lavish admiration and management money on introduced exotics that infest the waters of five continents.

When Milton and Cheadle travelled through what is now western Alberta, none of the streams that are now famous for their rainbow fishing had rainbows. The Bow and Crowsnest were full of bull trout and cutthroats. The Brazeau and North Saskatchewan had only bull trout.

Famous western rainbow trout streams are, almost without exception, artificial creations of modern technology. The famous rainbow and brown trout of Alberta's lower Bow River, for instance, do not belong there naturally. A series of dams control its water levels. Its abundant insect life depends on the City of Calgary's continuous supply of treated sewage effluent. Fishing the lower Bow for trophy browns and rainbows is healthy, outdoor exercise, but it's no more natural than hunting stocked pheasants in a cultivated grain field.

In the early 1900s, government agencies and local fish and game clubs released hatchery-raised trout into just about every accessible body of water in Alberta. Fishermen believed that a trout was a trout, and the more trout you stocked, the better the fishing would be. Fisheries biologists soon found that stocking trout actually reduces stream fishing quality. By the time they realized that native fish stocks thrive best in most streams, the zeal of the early stockers had hopelessly confused any effort to figure out what belonged where.

There was no doubt, however, that the dark little rainbows in the headwaters of the Athabasca River were not the product of some misguided early trout stocker. Milton's journal, written in the days before hatcheries, proved that.

Still, who cares about a trout's pedigree, anyway? Especially considering that the Athabasca rainbow is usually a stunted little guy, barely reaching ten inches in length before dying of old age. They are scrappy little fighters, admittedly, but hardly a sporting fish considering how easy they are to catch.

Carl Hunt, Alberta's fisheries biologist for the Edson district, disagrees with those sentiments on a couple of counts.

For one thing, he says, the idea that the Athabasca rainbows are a stunted race is just not true. "We took some out of one of the Tri-Creek streams," he says, "and put them into a little slough in the area where there was all kinds of food available but no hope of any fish surviving the winter."

Four-year-old trout — only six inches long when placed into the slough — grew to more than ten inches long by the time the biologists netted them again that fall. Hunt concludes that Athabasca rainbows are small simply because the habitat where they naturally occur does not give them the chance to grow large. Most native rainbows live in small headwater streams where food supplies are scant and the growing season may be less than three months.

In any case, he says, "Biologists and fishermen alike have come to see fishes as more than just so much aquatic protein."

Each native population of trout has evolved to fit the particular watershed and habitats in which it is found. The Athabasca rainbow is genetically distinct from the west coast rainbows stocked elsewhere in Alberta. It is the only rainbow trout that occurs naturally in waters flowing east from the Rockies, anywhere in North America. Uniquely suited to this place on the earth, the native Athabasca rainbow has an intrinsic right to exist.

It also has a complex and fascinating ecology that allows it to thrive in small forest streams.

When I caught my first Athabasca rainbow, I was struck by how different it looked from the silvery rainbows I was used to catching in the Maligne river, only a few miles away. The Maligne rainbows are stocked exotics. The rainbows in my little stream are dark and narrow, with slaty parr marks and an intense rainbow stripe along their sides. Their gill plates are a rich golden brown. They look like exactly the kind of trout that should live in shadowed streams that slip through dark forests of spruce and pine.

A species is much more than the sum of its chromosomes. The Athabasca rainbow is cold water, mossy stream banks littered with alder leaves and pine needles, flickering shade, the whine of mosquitoes, and the vast hush of Alberta's forested foothills. The Athabasca rainbow is tiny streams slipping over clean gravel, losing themselves in the roots of fallen spruce, then bubbling out into sunlit pools where mayflies bob and dance amid the splashy rises of hungry fish. The Athabasca rainbow is stunted, no matter what Carl Hunt may say about its potential to grow large, because habitat — at least as much as their genes — is what gives definition to real creatures.

Unfortunately, few fishermen take the time to reflect on what a trout really is, or on what values fishermen really get from fishing. Without reflection, it becomes too easy to reduce fishing to a matter of catching more, and bigger, fish than the next person. By those standards, the Athabasca rainbow will never stack up very well.

Biologist George Sterling found that a female rainbow produces only about 300 eggs each year in streams he studied south of Hinton. Even with good survival, very few fish hatch each year to replace the ones lost to fishing. A major flood can wipe out an entire generation.

"On unfished streams," says Carl Hunt, "we've found up to twelve hundred native rainbows per kilometre of stream. On most of the angled streams around Edson there's only two to three hundred per kilometre."

It does not take much fishing pressure to knock back the populations of so unproductive a fish. Fishing pressure comes with access, and the headwater streams of the McLeod, Athabasca, Wildhay and Berland have been opened up at an incredible rate during the last two decades. Coal exploration and development, oil and gas exploration and forestry operations have produced a maze of roads and cutlines. Few streams are free from fishing pressure.

Fortunately for the Athabasca rainbow, a female can mature and produce eggs when she is barely 5 1/2 inches long. Since few fishermen would keep a trout that small, even in the most heavily-fished streams a few spawners usually make it through each season to deposit their sparse load of eggs the next spring. Provincial regulation changes in 1987 improved prospects for the little natives, since anglers now have to release all trout less than seven inches in length. A seven-inch native rainbow is likely to be six years or older, and to have spawned three or four times.

The biggest threat to the native rainbows of the Athabasca River watershed, since the new regulations came into effect, is habitat loss. The small streams where the rainbows spawn are fragile environments. Old forests and undisturbed groundcover capture snow-melt and rainwater and release them gradually to the streams. Spring floods shift and redeposit the clean gravels at the tails of pools. In each stream there is an annual equilibrium to which the fish populations have adapted.

One new road can change that. In 1974 Champion Forest Products built a new logging road near Deerlick Creek, one of the Tri-Creek research streams. Up to eighteen times more silt and clay flushed into the stream during rainstorms after the company built the road.

All streams turn brown during the spring runoff, but spring floods flush most of the silt and clay on down the stream. When road cuts enable each summer rainstorm to wash raw sediments into the stream, however, the reduced summer flow is not strong enough to wash them away. Instead, silt and clay clog the fine gravel where trout eggs or fry develop, smothering the young fish.

Resource development brings roads. In the small corner of the world where Athabasca rainbows live, this means coal mining, logging and petroleum exploration. Most of the land east of Jasper National Park is committed to coal mining or pulp production.

Coal strip mines have operated in the headwaters of the Mcleod River since the early twentieth century. Sprawling open-pit mines have eradicated important rainbow trout streams and periodically dump catastrophic amounts of sediment into downstream reaches.

Logging companies occupy the rest of the landscape. In the late 1970s the Alberta government began actively promoting logging of the foothills around Hinton and Edson. A decade later, the government approved a huge pulp mill expansion. Logging requires a network of roads and landings, each feeding raw sediment into the once-clean streams where the native rainbows spawn. Each road also brings more fishermen to catch the adults.

The bad news does not stop there, either. Logging removes forests that formerly released water gradually into the trout streams. As forest cover disappears, the total water yield increases, but it also comes more frequently as major floods.

After trout spawn in late spring, the big June or July floods spilling off the clearcut landscape can wash away the spawning gravels and destroy the whole year's production. Major floods flushed George Sterling's research streams in 1969 and 1980. Both times, an entire generation of trout was destroyed. As floods become more frequent in the wake of logging, successful spawning seasons become rarer and rarer.

It's a grim picture. Logging and coal mining buy a lot more groceries than choosing to leave the wilds alone. The little forest trout may be well on their way to becoming victims — with the caribou and the grizzly — of a resource-based economy that creates short-term wealth out of long-term, massive landscape changes.

Hope, however, might come from the ecology of the

fish themselves. "One of the unique things about these rainbows," explains Carl Hunt, "is that they seem to thrive in real headwater, marginal habitats. In some of the places where we've found them overwintering, the riffles freeze right to the stream bed each winter and the trout are surviving in the little bits of water at the bottoms of a few deep pools."

Sedimentation and flooding inevitably grow worse further downstream. Perhaps a decade or two hence, if the streams that feed the upper Athabasca River become permanently disrupted by industrial forestry and mineral extraction, the dark little natives will still survive where headwater streams bubble out of muskegs before dropping to the gullied clearcuts below.

On the other hand, there may still be time to rein in the hasty industrialization of Alberta's boreal foothills. We could still choose to protect what healthy trout habitat remains, and to begin restoring that which we have damaged. If our remaining native fish populations are worth saving, then resource management should mean more than just dividing the spoils. A few unlogged, unroaded watersheds seem a small sacrifice to make, to maintain the dark native trout of the northern foothill forests.

The stream where I visit the little rainbows each summer is in a national park. Perhaps the fact that a park protects this one native rainbow stream is enough cause for hope. I don't think so. A national park, after all, is a kind of museum. What sort of society would insist that things of subtle value and beauty should only be found in museums?

The neglected rainbows of the northern foothills have thrived amid the forest shadows for millennia. They will continue to persist only if we — who came so recently and with such sudden impact — choose to protect the clear streams and ancient forests in which they dwell. ✕ *(1987)*

Medicine Trout

THE INDIANS CALLED IT Medicine Lake and seldom went there. They probably felt uneasy about the lake that disappeared each summer, while a raging river continued to pour into it.

Few later travellers chose to bushwhack the 21 kilometres of burnt timber and muskeg up from the Athabasca River valley. There was no particularly good reason to visit the place. In low water the lake was little more than an uninspiring mud-flat with a deep channel meandering through the middle. There were no fish in it at any season.

It was Maligne Lake, another sixteen kilometres up-valley that brought the first trail, and later the first road, to the weird lake with the sinkholes in the bottom. As with most of the lakes in the mountain national parks, improved access also brought a warden with a pack box full of trout fry. Stocking trout was one way in which the National Parks Service liked to add a little interest to the countryside.

It isn't clear when park wardens stocked the first trout in Medicine Lake. Nobody kept consistent records in those days. It appears, however, that Jasper National Park wardens stocked trout in 1928, 1929 and 1931. Starting in 1943, staff from the new fish hatchery at the mouth of the Maligne River released thousands of brook trout into Medicine Lake every few years. They released rainbows for the first time in 1966.

Both species did very well. The Maligne River, between Medicine and Maligne lakes, is full of spawning and rearing areas and teeming with stonefly nymphs and caddis larvae. So is Beaver Creek, which enters Medicine Lake from the east. No other native fish competed with the introduced trout for food and shelter. Maligne Lake, one of the largest lakes in the Rockies, was a vast unoccupied habitat. Medicine Lake provided a rich feeding area of silt-enriched flats full of mayfly nymphs, caddis larvae and midges.

Warden Gord Antoniuk considers the Maligne system one of the finest trout fisheries in western Canada. Many anglers agree. So many, in fact, that Park authorities have had to reduce catch limits and institute a no-bait rule to preserve this high-quality fishery.

I first fished Medicine Lake several years ago, when I still thought a bug was a bug and a fly was a Royal Coachman. I remember spending one frustrating afternoon wading along the deep-water channel and trying not to sink over the tops of my hip waders into glacial silt. The water virtually boiled with rising trout that were not the least interested in anything I had to offer them. Other anglers were catching them; I watched one gentleman take a five-pound rainbow on a dry fly. All I accomplished was to run out of tippet as I tried one fly after another, to no avail.

It was Lorne Currie, one of Jasper's fishing outfitters, who set me on the course that turned my fortunes. One winter I signed up for his fly-tying course so that I could finally get some use out of the fly-tying equipment I had bought several years earlier. Lorne showed me how to tie some of the flies that he uses most regularly in Jasper water. The books he introduced me to showed me how to use them more effectively. One book suggested that I try fishing an Adams, tied parachute style, on Medicine Lake.

Medicine Lake does not open for fishing until late summer. While driving past on my way to fish the upper Maligne River one August day, I noticed that fish were rising along the edge of Medicine Lake.

I pulled into a viewpoint, grabbed my gear, and slid down the bank to the lake shore. The lake was still full to the top of its basin so the water was no great distance down from the road. I tied on the Adams fly I had tied for this occasion. A trout rose a few feet from me, turned, and rose again. My hands began to shake.

A few gray mayflies were sailing on the wind-flecked surface. Now and then one whipped by on the stiff breeze blowing up from the Athabasca. Watching them sail off into the blue, I snagged a willow on the backcast and dropped a tangle of line only a couple yards from shore. Before I could recover all the slack, a fish took my fly. I reefed on the loose line with all my might to set the hook.

The reel screamed, the rod bent, and twenty yards out a silvery rainbow slashed out of the water, twisting and shaking. He took more line, and jumped again. He was getting well out into the lake. I looked at the reel. The backing was snaking out. My heart was pounding. I had not quite expected this kind of result so soon.

That one long run was enough for him. I gradually worked him back in to shore where I could net him. It was a beautiful deep-bellied rainbow, 18 inches long and 5 1/2 inches deep, with silvery sides and the deep mottled green back so characteristic of Medicine Lake rainbows.

It was a fluke, I told myself. You simply don't catch two pound rainbows from shore beside major tourist roads.

Just to be sure, I tried a few more casts. In an hour and a half I caught and released more than a dozen trout up to 15 inches in length. For some reason they were working the shallow water right along the shoreline.

Medicine Lake saw a lot of me that summer, although the fishing was rarely as good as that first day. For one thing, the lake is often windy. On many days it was pointless even to try casting cast a fly. For another thing, it seemed that the best action was between two and five in the afternoon; the rest of the time you could flail the water with every fly imaginable and not get a bite.

We all get obsessions from time to time in our lives; Medicine Lake soon became one for me.

Medicine is a strange lake with its swirling sinkholes at one end and roaring whitewater river at the other. Grizzlies and caribou occasionally stroll along the shoreline. Bighorn sheep watch from the roadside above. Each day the shoreline has changed and the fishing is full of new problems. Studying the lake, trying to figure out its mysteries, I have learned a lot about fish, fishing, and the sometimes fragile nature of a trout fishery. In fact, my days on Medicine Lake eventually changed my whole attitude toward fishing in national parks.

Medicine Lake is not a highly productive lake. The giant sinkholes that suck it almost dry each winter leave too little water to support weed beds. Wave action and constantly changing water level during the summer also keeps vegetation from developing. The channels get quite a pounding from wading fishermen in late fall. I suspect that the exposed lake bed, freezing solid each winter, must kill many of the insects that survive all the foot-traffic.

Nonetheless, the lake consistently produces good fly-fishing for rainbows up to four or five pounds, and the occasional brook trout. This is a self-sustaining fishery now, because Parks Canada no longer stocks fish. There is no need for stocking, anyway. The Maligne River and Beaver Creek, with their reliable water flows and abundant insect life, are perfect spawning and rearing areas for trout. The shallow expanse of Medicine Lake, too, produces abundant insect life each summer.

One of the most interesting of these insects accounted for the fish I caught along the shoreline in August. *Siphlonurus occidentalis*, the Western Gray Drake, is a peculiar little mayfly whose nymphs thrive in silty lake bottoms like that of

Medicine Lake. They burrow into the silt and feed on the organic debris that the Maligne River constantly flushes into the lake.

Come hatching time, the nymphs swim to shore, rather than rising to the surface. There they clamber out on a rock or some mud where the adult duns emerge from their nymphal shucks. As the nymphs and newly hatched adults congregate near the shore, cruising rainbows pick them off.

The sources I've checked don't agree on whether Gray Drake duns ever emerge in the water. I suspect that one reason the Adams is so successful on Medicine Lake is that the vast stretches of shallow-water habitat result in a lot of the nymphs hatching before they can reach dry land. During most hatches, a scattering of duns float on the surface. The trout take them with gusto.

Nevertheless, if the Gray Drake makes Medicine Lake a fine fly-fishing lake, it might also introduce a sort of Catch-22. As the lake drops in late summer, fishers begin to wade across the silty flats to fish the deep-water channel in the middle. Sometimes the whole upper lake is a web of tracks and trails from the foot traffic across the flats. Nobody has ever studied what effect this kind of traffic has on the mayfly nymphs in their delicate little burrows. It may help explain the complaints by some longtime anglers about disappointingly sparse mayfly hatches in recent years.

Some anglers have also begun to comment that the average size of fish caught has decreased in recent years. As park warden Gord Antoniuk points out, though, when many fishermen are killing limits of trout, something has to give. "You can't keep killing spawners and expect the fishery to hold up," he says. "Every lake has a breaking point."

Stocking is not an option. Parks Canada got out of that business years ago when biologists realized that exotic fish stocks had created lasting damage in streams and lakes that once contained only native fish. Besides, the Maligne system produces thousands of trout each year. They just do not get a chance to grow big when too many anglers kill fish.

Lorne Currie advocates catch-and-release for Medicine Lake. In 1985, the Jasper Fish and Game Association sponsored a resolution calling for reduced limits. The fishery may be limited to single-hook artificial lures in the future. "Generally, bait-caught fish suffer higher mortality when fishermen try to release fish," says Gord Antoniuk.

Since the same core of keen anglers catches most of Medicine Lake's trout, a non regulatory solution is already available. Anglers need only limit ourselves, rather than wait for the government to do it for us. Restraint is an underrated virtue that would solve many conservation problems. Restraint, among anglers privileged to enjoy Medicine Lake's fishery, might lead those anglers to walk on each others' tracks and seek other ways to reduce their impact on trout habitat.

I used to set a two-fish limit for myself in the Maligne system. Now I catch my eating trout in stocked waters. I save Medicine Lake for the sheer enjoyment of catch-and-release and the challenge of figuring out trout habitat and foods. Lately I have stopped wading the mudflats; now I haul my canoe down the embankment and float the channel. As my respect for this place has grown, I have become more demanding of myself. I want to be worthy of Medicine Lake.

Perhaps fishing in national parks should be different from fishing everywhere else. Maybe angling in such highly valued landscapes should be more a form of nature study with a hook than a way to put food on the table. Maybe these are the places where anglers can best study to learn restraint, humility and respect.

Medicine Lake is where I first began to contemplate

that possibility. It is only one of countless lakes and streams throughout Jasper and the other national parks. These are all special places, by definition. Fishing here could be a way by which anglers study to belong, not strive to take. If that is true, then it is by far the most important thing I have learned while fishing Medicine Lake. ⁎ *(1986)*

The Flower of Fishes

THE SMOKY RIVER drops from its sources in the glaciers of the continental divide from one wild rapid to another. It emerges from its wilderness headwaters as a broad, gray waterway winding along the bottom of a deep valley incised into the agricultural plain of Alberta's Peace River country.

For the most part its tributaries are smaller versions of the Smoky. They are mountain-bred and volatile, turning brown and thunderous after each summer freshet, filling the valleys with the roar and crash of hurrying water. Their cold temperatures and silt-clouded water combine with dramatic flow fluctuations to limit the productivity of their fisheries. Bull trout, whitefish and some Arctic grayling dwell there, but few anglers ply their waters.

The Little Smoky, however, is different. It is a humble stream, fed by muskeg springs, meandering from one long pool to another through a wilderness of spruce and tamarack; caribou and wolves. Since it arises from a heavily-forested watershed rather than the high mountains, it floods less frequently and violently than other tributaries. Its stream bed is more stable and its fishery more productive than other nearby streams.

Even with four-wheel drive an angler can only drive to

within three miles of its upper reaches. Its quiet chatter goes unheard most days. Its weed beds and gravel runs shelter grayling, bull trout and whitefish that have never tasted the sting of an angler's hook. It is a quiet river in a quiet valley, unnoticed and rarely visited.

It has only two real claims to fame: it is one of the last intact watersheds left in the Alberta foothills, and it may be the finest Arctic grayling stream in Canada.

The province's regional fisheries biologist, Carl Hunt, has measured a catch rate of six to ten grayling per angler hour on the Little Smoky. "We have a set of standards that we use to judge the productivity of different fisheries," he says. "For a stocked trout lake, for example, we expect about 0.5 trout per angler hour. For perch, it goes up to 0.7 per angler hour. Carson Lake, one of our best rainbow trout lakes, produces between one and two fish per angler hour. So you can see where the Little Smoky stands."

Darryl Smith, a Valleyview, Alberta angler, is a Zone Director for the Alberta Fish and Game Association. Smith says that the river, "…contains the finest Arctic Grayling fishing in Alberta, and it would be difficult to find finer fishing anywhere in North America."

Smith recently submitted a management proposal to Alberta's Department of Forestry, Lands and Wildlife. It contained recommendations aimed at perpetuating this threatened wilderness fishery.

"The western Athabasca River watershed is the most southerly distribution of Arctic Grayling in Canada," he points out. "The watershed had good access developed in the 1960s and 1970s and grayling populations are a fraction of their former levels. Many people recall the glory days of the '50s and '60s when catches of 100 fish or more were common. Lying immediately north of the Athabasca is the Little Smoky River watershed which remains the farthest south quality grayling fishery in North America."

In 1988, the Alberta government, caught up in the enthusiasm that attends each boom cycle in the pulp and paper industry, approved several new pulp mills in the western part of the province. To provide timber for the new mills, they have put the entire Little Smoky watershed on the block. As part of this heavily subsidized new forestry development, the government has already begun cutting new, high-quality roads into the area. Oil and gas exploration companies, meanwhile, continue to punch cutlines down to the river's edge. Many hunters and fishermen use the seismic lines to travel deeper into the wilds on all-terrain vehicles.

For the first time in Alberta's history, however, fishery managers took steps to preserve a high-quality fishery before problems developed. Historically, the regulations remained generous until well after the fishery had begun to fall apart. Effective in 1989, the upper Little Smoky River was designated a catch-and-release fishery — the first such designation aimed at conserving Arctic grayling in Canada. Darryl Smith's initiative may be paying off.

Early in 1988, Carl Hunt told me he and his technicians were planning a trip to the Little Smoky. They needed accurate population numbers so that Carl would be able to evaluate the success of the new regulations. He also needed to know how widely the grayling travel within the stream. When Carl told me that — in order to tag the fish — they had to angle for them with fly rods, I asked him if he needed any help. Who could resist helping the cause of science under those circumstances?

On August 9, 1988, I met Carl Hunt and Rudy Hawryluk at Edson, halfway between Edmonton and Jasper. Their four-wheel drive truck, with a trailer containing two all-terrain vehicles, was waiting in front of the Fish and Wildlife office when I arrived.

We headed north into the forested foothills that stretch along the northern flank of the Rockies and merge to the north and east with the vast forests of northern Canada. The forest was endless, the sky was endless, and great dark thunderstorms dragged grey sheets across the hills. The rain storms occasionally intersected with our route, turning stretches of the gravel road into slime that threatened to swallow my little station wagon.

Three and a half hours out of Edson my car was caked with mud and I was growing a tad weary of oil development roads and rain. At the Berland Fire Tower Road, Carl and Rudy stopped and Carl walked back to me.

"The road gets bad from here in," he said. This was news to me. I thought the road had been bad for the last three hours. "You'd better leave your car here and come the rest of the way in the 4X4."

We ground and jolted our way along a summer seismic line for another nine miles. Finally, we spotted a wall tent on the skyline. The rest of Carl's crew had started a day earlier and pitched camp where we would not miss it — right in the middle of the road. The camp was deserted.

It was six in the evening. At this latitude that meant it wouldn't get dark for another four hours. We decided to head down to the river rather than wait for the others to get back.

The camp was right on the drainage divide between the Berland and Little Smoky Rivers. As we set out for the river, I looked out on a sight that has become rare in most of Canada and the United States: an unbroken sea of old-growth timber. Huge spruce and balsam fir grow on the better-drained slopes, with understories of alder, cow parsnip and horsetail. On more gentle slopes the big timber gives way to muskeg — sphagnum bogs with lichen-draped tamaracks and black spruce. Moose and caribou feed and shelter in the muskeg and share the floodplain meadows with grizzly bears, elk and mule deer.

We bounced and jolted on the ATVs down a grown-over gas well road and through a mile of muskeg. As we drew near the river, the muskeg gave way to willow tangles and meadows of tall grass. At length we emerged in a clearing among several huge spruce. The gentle chatter of running water rose to meet us.

The Little Smoky was quieter than I had imagined. We stopped beside a long pool. It was shallow and weedy, punctuated with strips of clear water the colour of weak tea. Rising fish dimpled the surface.

The others had tagging gear to prepare, so I rigged my rod and tied on a black ant. At my second cast, a fish jumped clear out of the water and intersected solidly with the hook.

It jumped twice and fought with short, powerful runs. As I recovered line, I caught my first sight of the fish. Its huge dorsal fin was rimmed with a band of turquoise blue and covered with a scattering of red spots. Its body had a purple tinge and its pectoral fins were tiger-striped in black and white. Fins erect, quivering with vivid life, it dashed for the bottom in brief flurries, then jumped again at my feet. I lifted it gently from the water and shook it off the hook into Carl's holding net.

For fifteen minutes we caught one grayling after another. I had never seen fishing like it before; the fish ranged in size up to fourteen inches and took dry flies with gusto. No matter how many we caught in a pool, the others remained no less willing to rise. At one point, a fish took Rudy's lure as it trailed in the water right beside him.

Once the net was full, Rudy and Carl measured and tagged the occupants. Each tag was an inch-long fluorescent orange tube with a number on it. As the biologists released each fish, it would ease down to the river bed to sulk briefly, sometimes right beside our feet.

"The fish of the future," I said.

Carl looked puzzled.

I pointed at two grayling resting beside him, orange tags trailing behind their dorsal fins. "Built-in strike indicators," I said. He grimaced.

It felt wrong to attach the plastic tags to wild fish in such remote and unspoiled wilderness. We all knew, however, that little of value survives untouched for long in twentieth-century North America. The road crews were already at work. The future was on its way to the Little Smoky. I hoped that the efforts of Carl and his crew — and of committed individuals like Darryl Smith — would shape a different future for this river than what has already befallen so many other grayling fisheries.

The Arctic grayling represents a strange dichotomy of values among the angling fraternity. We both revere and squander it.

Linnaeus, who made his life's work the naming of every living thing he could get his hands on dead examples of, called the grayling *Thymallus thymallus*. The Latin name refers to the suggestion of thyme in a freshly-caught grayling's characteristic odour. Many great angling writers have spoken of it with respect. In fact, the first reference to the artificial fly in writing was by the Roman rhetorician Aeolian concerning the grayling. St. Ambrose, the bishop of Milan in fourth-century Italy, described the grayling as "the flower of fishes." Roderick Haig-Brown called it "Poisson bleu" for its translucent mix of purples, blues and reds. He also called it the standard-bearer, or Thymallus signifer, preferring this scientific name for a fish whose huge, elegantly shaped dorsal fin is so much a part of its beauty.

In spite of its renown and respect as a creature of subtle beauty that rises readily to the dry fly, fights nobly and occupies the finest of wilderness streams, humans have nonetheless exploited and abused the grayling during the last two centuries. Over much of its original range, the grayling has been extinct for many years.

The famous Au Sable River was only one of several Michigan streams that supported large grayling populations during the frontier era. In a privately published book on Michigan's fish, Harold Smedley described how fishermen would mine the spawning runs, filling "...the box of a common lumber wagon full of fish, not just one load but half a dozen each spring for several successive years. All sizes were taken; the larger were kept, the fingerlings thrown on the bank to rot."

The Michigan grayling Smedley described is extinct. The lumberjack and the great log drives that ruined their rivers doomed those that survived the fish hogs of the frontier.

Grayling were also native to the headwaters of the Missouri River. Montana grayling now thrive only in the headwaters of the Big Hole River.

In Canada, many grayling fisheries declined over the past century because of a combination of too much access and too little restraint among anglers. Grayling are fish of the frontier, and meat-hunting is a time-honoured frontier tradition. Grayling take flies, spinners and bait enthusiastically; as a result they are quickly fished out.

Carl explained that grayling reach sexual maturity only after they are ten or eleven inches in length. Consequently, many see the bottom of a frying pan before they see their first spawning season. Many anglers keep and kill fish as small as six or eight inches in length. In the first real attempt to conserve grayling populations in increasingly accessible Alberta streams, the provincial government imposed a 12-inch minimum size restriction in 1986. Catch-and-release for the Little Smoky represents a further step, aimed at not only maintaining the fishery, but protecting its trophy quality.

Darryl Smith feels that the government should take another step to show the Little Smoky the respect so rare a river deserves. The Alberta Wilderness Association recently took up his proposal to set aside the entire upper watershed of the river as a protected wilderness. Alberta has set aside no large wilderness areas in the foothills or boreal regions. Protecting the Little Smoky from roads and machinery would do more than preserve grayling habitat. It would assure future anglers of the opportunity to rediscover the stillness and wildness of the original north.

Darryl Smith considers the Little Smoky to be unique because of both "...the high density and record size of the fish in the population. Fish exceeding 50 centimetres (19 inches) are taken each year and it is probable that some of these would be new provincial records if they were officially registered."

Of the sixty or seventy grayling I released, none was more than sixteen inches long. The following day we fished for several hours, wandering upstream from pool to pool, catching, tagging and releasing fish after fish. Besides grayling we caught mountain whitefish and bull trout, both native species. No one has ever introduced exotics into the Little Smoky watershed — yet another feature that makes this river a rarity among North American watersheds.

At one pool I stopped to study the tracks of deer, elk and wolf on a point bar. The cries of an osprey caught my attention and I looked up to see it diving repeatedly at a bald eagle. Both species are common along the river, as are mergansers, kingfishers, river otters and other fish-eaters. The high density of grayling sustains an ecosystem more similar to what one might expect to find along a coastal salmon stream than a boreal river.

The grayling fed all day, although the fishing occasionally tapered off after we had taken several fish from a pool. They rested on the bottom of the pools rather than hanging in the water column like feeding trout. Rising for a dry fly, they had to race to the surface before the fly drifted away. The result was quick rolling rises that often carried the grayling right out of the water — spectacular fishing. Immediately upon being hooked, they would make a downstream run; upstream fishing was an exercise in frantic stripping and missed strikes.

The two crews tagged well over 150 Arctic grayling during my brief stay. After chugging back up the cutline to camp on the second day, it was time for me to leave. When I arrived at my station wagon, I felt like I was awakening from a dream. I shook hands with Carl, got into the car and drove off, reentering the twentieth century from a valley that time seems to have forgotten.

Behind me, night was pooling beneath the ancient forests of the Little Smoky watershed. In shallow pools where bats flickered overhead and water crowfoot flowers winked back, the grayling were no doubt dimpling the surface and sipping mayfly nymphs from the gravel. Perhaps a wolf was lapping from the river or standing on a gravel bar, testing the wind for the rumour of caribou or moose in the nearby muskeg.

I was leaving the Little Smoky's hidden wilderness and schools of delicate grayling behind. I had glimpsed, too briefly, the kind of wilderness fishing that, in far too many places, resides only in the past.

I will be back. When I return, I hope sincerely to find the Little Smoky unchanged, its tea-coloured water still slipping over clear gravel riffles to pause in weedy eddies or darken in deep clear pools where schools of grayling eye the surface, waiting for a passing fly. I hope I will be able again to stand beside the river and hear only water-chatter and wind, and the long slow silence of the living wild. I believe I will. ❧ *(1988)*

The Hunt

Environmental Education

NORTH OF CALGARY, where 4th Street's pavement gave way at last to gravel, there used to be a quiet little creek valley full of cows, gophers, and silver willows. A few cottonwoods grew by the creek. Sometimes a farm truck rattled by, but for the most part the valley was an empty sort of place in summer. Few people gave the little valley a second look. If they had, they might have seen a kid getting an environmental education.

I found the place because, when hunting season ended, my father found other things to do with his Saturdays. Much to my regret, I was on my own until fishing season began in the spring.

Dad introduced each of his kids to the outdoors as soon as we could walk fast enough to keep up with him. I could never get enough of those precious Saturdays. We hunted weedy irrigation ditches east of Strathmore for pheasants or hiked game trails and cutlines into hidden foothills creeks to fish for cutthroat trout.

By the time I was ten my identity was already steeped in the smell of autumn stubble, the evening whistle of passing mallards, the possibility of moose and bear. I was addicted. I couldn't get enough of the world beyond the city that my father's hunting and fishing trips revealed to me.

However, kids have more spare time than dads. When hunting season ended I faced the prospect of weekends without the wilds. I stuffed my pockets with stones and went looking for pheasants down along the railway tracks. There weren't too many there, but I spotted some birds I didn't know. Mom got me a bird book. Next weekend I went looking for more birds, becoming increasingly amazed to discover how many other kinds of wild things lived out there in the real world.

Come summer, bird book and lunch tucked in a haversack, I bicycled out of the city into new adventures. That was how I discovered Beddington Creek.

It was a valley like those where we hunted pheasants, but close enough to the city that I could get there on my own in an hour or two. On my first visit I found a marsh hawk nest in some buckbrush. Next time I found a pair of western kingbirds sharing a nest tree with a pair of ferruginous hawks. It was poor planning on both parts. Every time the hawks tried to return with another gopher for their hungry chicks, the kingbirds would launch an aerial attack on the hawks. Both pairs of birds must have had a miserable summer. I watched, fascinated.

One thing led to another. I still hunt, fish and watch birds, and now I have kids myself.

But Beddington Creek valley is gone. Calgary devoured it while I wasn't looking.

Last year I agreed to give a talk on nature and writing to elementary students in three northeast Calgary schools. It was only when I arrived at the first school that I realized my quiet valley had become city; the school stood right in the middle of it. I saw no hawks.

The students were eager and attentive. I asked how many went fishing or hunting with their parents. A couple hands showed. The rest did not. I asked them questions about nature. The answers were naive, hopeful, and obviously based on television shows. Some slides in my talk included scenes from hunting trips. The kids were clearly uneasy with them.

Beddington Creek — its hawks, kingbirds, silver willows and pheasants — is buried beneath a sterile urban cityscape. So, too, are most of the kids in Calgary, Saskatoon, Edmonton, Vancouver and the other cities that now contain most western Canadians.

A friend describes modern Canadians as growing up "orphaned from Nature." In the Beddington Creek valley that day, his description seemed doubly apt.

The schools I visited, like many other western Canadian schools, have environmental education programs. In spite of excellent learning resources, however, most are taught in artificial settings by teachers with no real understanding of nature. Few of the students in those classes have ever had the chance to develop personal bonds with the wild. They learn about ozone holes and atmospheric change and pesticides, as if the environment is simply a mess of hopeless problems. They do not learn what a pheasant track looks like in the snow, or how the sun looks through a swarm of hatching mayflies, or how it feels to sit on a mountainside with a rifle on your lap, talking lazily with an adult who listens.

The most effective environmentalists I have known balanced depth of experience and breadth of knowledge with a deep emotional commitment to places they loved. This suggests to me that environmental education cannot just be about knowledge. Children are creatures of experience. They need to bond not only to the people but to the places in their lives too. Childhood should be about learning to care, experiencing the dance of life, and filling one's heart with that burning ache that comes from being in, and of, wild nature. Later, there will be time enough to learn about environmental problems.

I suspect that those who understand life, death and the value of wild places from having bonded to nature while bonding with an adult, ultimately receive the most valuable environmental education. They are the ones who will care enough, and understand enough, to fight to protect habitat. They will have the personal insights that will enable them to challenge simplistic solutions to environmental problems, and come up with ideas that might work. They are the people most likely to give nature, hunting, fishing and wild places a tomorrow.

I fear that there are too few of them.

Recently, Gail and I made a deal with our kids. For each kind of bird, mammal, amphibian or fish that they identified during the year, they would get a dollar to spend on a book. Then we took them hiking, fishing and hunting, and left the rest up to them. It cost a few bucks, but we knew we would be buying them books anyway. Already they are learning, on their own, to find, recognize and delight in the vast diversity of living things that comprise the West's rich, natural heritage.

Last evening, Katie asked me to take her out to look for animals.

At dusk we stood above an autumn-gold marsh listening to the clamour of Canada geese as a dozen or so elk, statue-still, stood clustered in the shallow water. A six-point bull splashed through the shallows, stretching out his neck to bugle. Then the whole herd turned suddenly and stampeded across the marsh, through the sedge fringe, into the aspens. The geese vanished into cloud-shadow, and the world stood still and breathless.

I looked at my nine-year-old daughter, standing spellstruck beside me.

I thought of those kids in Calgary.

I wondered why nobody had ever taken them hunting, or fishing. I wondered, too, what it will mean to things like Canada geese, elk and autumn marshes if the next generation grows up without adults who will take them as deep as they can go into the real world beyond the pavement. ⁂ *(1995)*

Memories on the Water

This hunting story ends with a trout. I'm not sure where it begins.

Let's say that it begins three years ago. That is when I moved back to Jasper and resumed my quest for a trophy ram among the headwaters of the McLeod River.

The search for a trophy ram is generally a long one. Some hunters never do find one. Before a ram can be legally shot, he has to have survived at least five or six hunting seasons — more than long enough to learn the meaning of the sudden burst of human activity late each alpine summer. The rams — especially the really big ones that have lived nine or more years — are few. Confounding the whole business further is the fact that sheep hunting has become very popular lately. Getting a sheep today is almost as much a matter of outracing the competition as it is one of finding the sheep in the first place.

Nevertheless, it gets in the blood.

Each summer I donned my pack and hiking boots and picked my way up through sultry, resin-scented timberline forests to glass and study the headwater basins. Each summer I spotted rams, including the occasional huge old-timer. And each summer, a day or two before hunting season, the rams evaporated into thin air as an army of hopeful sheep hunters arrived to do their last minute scouting. The past two opening days have found me picking berries. Hunting seemed pointless.

Most successful hunters find their sheep during the first or last three days of the season. Such statistics left me cold; my reasons for hunting the high country for sheep had more to do with solitude than success. I soon found myself hunting in midseason when the odds were poorest but the competition also scarcest. Alone with the wild, I bellied up to windswept ridges to glass hidden basins, or hiked along shadowed cutlines in the eerie, pre-dawn stillness, trying to reach far valleys in time to spot sheep still feeding. Mid season hunting allowed me to have the wind and scenery to myself. I could become wholly absorbed in the search for a ram rather than distracted by worries about other hunters.

When I finally spotted my ram, one early October day, he was in a snowy opening where the last stunted timber gave way to snow-covered, windswept rubble. He was alone and seemingly at peace, looking for all the world as if he were not even aware the hunting season was open.

All rational thought vanished from my mind. The mountain had finally seen fit to present me with a ram. All the long days, hard climbs and futile glassing had finally paid off. I didn't stop to plan my stalk — I just noted the lay of the land and plunged into the forest. The ram was out of sight, but I could see a big gully that should take me within a hundred yards of him.

It was hard going. The slope had been burned fifty or sixty years ago. Young pines were crowded together in a jungle of crisscrossed deadfall. Everything was slippery with melting snow, but adrenaline leant wings to my feet. Climbing had never seemed so easy.

Wet from the waist down from melting snow, sweating with exertion, I stopped at the edge of the timber. I leaned against a fallen log to catch my wind.

To the west, the mountains formed a wall of white, broken with strips of dark timber and melt-stained cliffs. Through the binoculars I could see sheep trails crisscrossing snow-covered talus slides. Far up a side valley forty ewes were feeding on a windswept ridge. An eagle sailed past, wings set and eyes searching. Wind roared and seethed in the pine forest below.

Rested, I moved on, alert now. Above, the slopes were

blindingly bright in the late afternoon sunlight.

A young ram emerged from the timber, moving up-slope about seventy yards to my right. A ewe and lamb appeared behind him. I wondered if the wind had given me away, but they seemed unconcerned. I waited. No more appeared.

Another few steps and I was in the open. To my dismay, none of the landmarks I had noted from below looked the same up here. Undecided, I looked around to find a route that would give me the best field of view.

Then the ram stood up. He was less than a hundred yards straight above me. He stared at me, concerned but not yet alarmed. I settled the crosshairs on his chest, surprised at how steady my hold was after so hard a climb, and squeezed. The ram dropped, rolled, and came to rest against a fallen tree.

I had my ram. Yet somehow, even as I leaned my gun against my pack and sat beside him, silently thanking the mountain for its gift, it seemed unreal. Something in the back of my mind nagged at me. It felt like an anticlimax of some kind; as if I had missed the point of something.

A hunting season consists of many different things. Three weeks later I was in a different landscape, carrying a different gun. This time I had a twelve-gauge shotgun, one barrel loaded with a deer slug and the other with number 7 ′ shot.

The deer slug was more wishful thinking than anything else. Although the mountains to the west were still white with snow, down here on the aspen sidehills along the Wildhay River the ground was dry as a bone. Dead leaves crackled like potato chips with each step, the whitetail rut was still two weeks away, and I was little more likely to see a buck than I was to spot an elephant.

Grouse, however, were another story. Something in the crisp morning air had the ruffed grouse cocks thinking of spring. Every so often I would hear one drum hopefully in the undergrowth. It was wonderful hunting, wandering through the golden glory of a foothills autumn from spruce grove to aspen bluff to willow tangle, following the drums of autumn.

By midmorning, with three birds in my pack and the sun high in the sky, the drumming had ended. After half an hour or so, I stopped at the edge of a grove of spruce and gave the situation some thought. Maybe the grouse needed a little encouragement.

I thumped my chest once, then again, then faster, ending in a drum roll. A little sheepish, I looked around to make sure I was alone.

A grouse replied from the shadows under the spruce — it had worked! I eased forward, peering into the tangles of deadfall and rose bushes.

The grouse began to peep nervously, getting ready to flush. I strained my eyes; where was the little skulker?

With that heart-stopping roar of wings that no hunter has ever gotten used to, the grouse exploded from the underbrush and rocketed into the alders by the river. More out of instinct than any conscious hope, I swung and shot as he disappeared into the foliage.

The day was shocked into silence by the shotgun blast. At length, a squirrel chattered somewhere. The river gossiped quietly to itself beyond the alders, and just for a moment I thought I heard a faint fluttering.

I couldn't have hit him; I hardly even saw him. Just in case, though, I forced my way into the shrubbery where the bird had disappeared. Wings and tail fanned in death, the ruffed grouse lay on the bank of the river.

I sat against a tree and dug out my thermos. I lay the grouse in a row on the grass and studied them. Again, that vague feeling assailed me of having missed something. This was already one of my best grouse hunts ever — a beautiful morning and four birds in hand — and I felt strangely unconnected with it.

Fall is a strange season, both melancholy and content, a time when summer dies in a sudden blaze of glory. Animals grown fat on summer's green wealth wait unconcerned for the slow starvation of another bitter winter. It is a time when all of nature is abundant, but it is also the end of abundance. It is the time of the hunting moon, and as all hunters know, it is too short.

In November I visited Dad. We shot a few sharp-tailed grouse and a buck whitetail. The slopes turned brown and dull. Trees stood naked in the wind. When the first big storm of winter ushered in the end of another golden season afield, we had good meat in the freezer and the warmth of new memories.

It had been memorable and fine. Somehow, too, it had been incomplete.

That winter, as I sat at my fly-tying bench, I dug out the ruffed grouse skins I had saved after that beautiful day on the Wildhay. Then I cut scraps from the hide of the ram I had shot high above the headwaters of the McLeod River and tied some trout flies.

I found those flies peculiarly satisfying. Intricately patterned in the same browns and creams as the leaves and logs of the forest floor, the rump and shoulder feathers of the ruffed grouse made an elegant Matuka-style wing. The dark hairs of the ram's foreleg flared and spun beautifully into a muddler-style head. The finished fly was something new, my own invention. I knew it would become something special.

Aboriginal hunters filled medicine bags with scraps and pieces of things that had special significance to them. I built my new fly the same way. I had a feeling that when the time came to baptize it, something memorable might happen.

One day I tied a grouse and ram matuka muddler onto

a whisper-thin tippet. After carefully wetting it, I dropped it gently on the edge of a riffle on a stream whose name, for reasons obvious to any serious angler, eludes me right now. It disappeared into the current. The swing of the line marked its drift as it slipped deep into a dark and mysterious place under the far bank.

Only the irrefutable certainty that such a hole must hold a big trout had convinced me to try one of my little beauties. Until I stood beside this pool, I had always preferred just to look at them and remember the hunts that had yielded them.

The line stopped, then jerked upstream. I reared back and set the hook into something heavy and sullen. The rod throbbed in my hand. Something golden flashed deep in the pool's swirling shadows. Then the reel screamed and the line sliced suddenly downstream into tailwater.

The autumn world vanished as the fish struggled at the end of my line. Everything was water, light, shade, the pull of the trout against the rod in my hand, the seesawing of line…and at length the trout was finished. It slid, barely resisting, into the shallows and managed only a couple of weak flops as I dragged it, heavy and glistening, onto the streamside grass.

I do not know what it weighed — maybe four or five pounds. It was a brown trout, tea-coloured and golden like the stream that produced it. It was as long as my forearm.

I shook the fly from the big trout's lip and slid him gently back into the water. He started to tilt sideways but I steadied him, holding him so that water washed into his mouth and out through his gills. His sides grew firmer in my hands as strength returned. Then he gave a powerful twist and burrowed away into the secret depths of his pool.

It's one thing about fishing, I thought, as I made myself comfortable on the stream bank and dug in my creel for a deer meat sandwich. When you hunt, success is final. A shot animal or bird is dead. You can't let it go. Fishing, you can have your cake and eat it too.

I blew the fly dry. It didn't look any worse for wear. In my fly book I had more grouse and ram matuka muddlers, and a couple made from sharptail feathers and deer hair.

It is funny how things work out. I had not held a gun in my hands for months. Yet only now by the chattering little central Alberta stream, with the scent of an old brown trout still on my hands and a vireo singing tirelessly in the poplar foliage overhead, was last fall's hunting season finally complete. Its whole essence had been distilled into a few lures of feather and hair, and the strange satisfaction of having hunted, held, and released a great trout.

Coming home with something dead does not a hunt make. Looking at the little matuka fly, I remembered the high windy country where the ram had lived. I recalled the first sight of the old monarch quietly studying the valley slopes below, the drumming of grouse on a golden October day in the aspen woods, the far soughing of wind in pines....The long winter had filtered my hunting memories, leaving only the best behind, woven like magic into the matuka muddlers I had crafted during the long winter nights. Maybe there was medicine in those flies. Maybe that was what prompted the strange impulse that made me release a fish, the likes of which I may never see again, rather than keep and kill it, and take it home.

I wove my memories into lures and cast them in the water. They caught a fish, and I released him. In releasing that fish I affirmed something I had always known but never understood — that hunting is more a celebration and affirmation of life and beauty, than the pursuit of death. I think I am beginning, now, to understand the reasons why I hunt. ❧ *(1987)*

One day, as we ate our lunch high above a headwater valley, Bill Tilleman told me about his first encounter with a wolf. He had been hunting elk on the upper Red Deer River, on a grassy mountaintop with sheltered gullies and isolated stands of timber. Bill and his partner had separated after a hard climb. Bill was just strolling over a rise when he came face to face with a big grey wolf trotting up the other side.

"I was so close I could see the shock in his eyes when he saw me, and the contraction of his leg muscles as he put on the brakes. I could almost feel his horror at blundering into me."

The wolf, barely ten yards away, recovered instantly. Flipping end for end, it streaked away across the alpine tundra.

His partner demanded to know afterwards why he had not shot it. "It never even occurred to me," he said. "I was too awestruck. I couldn't have shot him."

If Bill had not been elk hunting that day, he would have had no story to tell. Nobody would ever hear the delight in his voice when he recalls the experience.

His story got me thinking of one of my own elk-hunting adventures that took place high on a mountain ridge in southern Alberta. I had set out at four in the morning to reach the high country before daybreak. I arrived in a howling wind storm on the long summit ridge just as the sun began to show above the flat rim of the distant prairie.

I was working my way along the ridge, leaning against the wind and scanning the shadowed meadows for feeding elk, when I saw a small bird flying up the lee slope toward me. As it crested the ridge, the wind hit it head-on. It dropped near the ground, wings beating hard, barely making headway as it fought its way into the Chinook.

It was the first of a long flock of rosy finches — small mountain birds that nest in cliff faces and forage in the alpine meadows. As they crossed the ridge, several passed within inches of me, working hard but progressing with painful slowness. Their bright little eyes watched me until they made it past and could dive away down the windward side of the ridge. The birds glowed a brilliant rose in the rays of the rising sun.

I stood, entranced, in the middle of a strange, slow-motion dance.

The image has stayed with me ever since — a strange and privileged experience that I earned by not being at home in a warm bed where most people are at four a.m. on an October day.

Later that fall I got my first elk on that ridge. Nevertheless, the most vivid image that remains is of those tiny birds, glowing in the sunrise, fighting their way over the ridge. I could have reached out and touched them.

When non-hunters challenge us to justify our pastime, their criticism usually focuses on the fact that we kill things. Indeed, when we plan our trips and head out in the morning, most hunters do focus on the desire to bring home prey. Still, as any real hunter knows, a dead thing does not a successful hunt make, any more than an empty freezer equals a wasted fall.

Bill and my brother Gordon are both serious hunters. I can recall each deciding, on different trips when we finally found bighorn sheep after long days of scouting, not to go after them. They had already found what they sought.

Out there in the hills and plains, strange and wonderful things happen every day. Eagles play in the updrafts.

Martens hurry along fallen logs. Chickadees mine dead bark for moth eggs. Wild things mate and play and die. Sun and clouds paint an endlessly changing mosaic across the spectacular landscapes and wildlands of the West. The real and natural universe continues to unfold in all the glory and complexity of Creation.

Who is there to witness it?

We are.

Hunters are witnesses in the wild. Our passion drives us to rise early in the cold, dark hours of the dawn. We often travel many miles to lose ourselves in favourite landscapes that resonate in our souls. Although we may start with friends or family, at some point we find ourselves alone. We move quietly, totally involved with small breezes, undergrowth, the hidden places in the vegetation, and the vast, overarching sky.

Hunters become predators, and thus one with the ecosystem — no longer outsiders or interested observers, but full participants. We are there, wholly and completely, and open to what will come.

So it is that we sometimes come home at season's end with our tags unfilled, but our hearts overflowing. A successful hunt does not require a kill, only the possibility of one. It is that possibility that places us out in the heart of the living wild where wolves trot casually over alpine ridges, small birds drag the sunrise into the wind, and bighorn sheep survey the wilderness from hollowed-out beds on high talus slopes.

Sometimes we ourselves forget what those who do not hunt cannot understand: that it is not merely the kill that makes us hunters. It is the witnessing, the being there, and those intimate moments of belonging when the living world reveals itself to those who work so hard to become a part of it.

That is why we will be there again next fall in the cold and the rain and the snow, working hard to penetrate the most secret of wild places. We are not seeking death. We are actively participating in, and celebrating, the incredible richness of life. ❧ *(1993)*

High Country: The Rockies

Bow Corridor: Heart of a Mountain Ecosystem

LATE IN JUNE, the Bow Corridor lies sodden beneath heavy, gray clouds. The mountaintops are hidden from view. Rain slants down onto the streets of Canmore and Exshaw, splatters into aspen foliage along the lower slopes of Mount Yamnuska, and lashes the face of Lac des Arcs.

It is the kind of day when people stay at home and complain about the weather. The tires of passing trucks and cars on the Trans-Canada Highway hiss and whine. Through the slap-slap of windshield wipers, the travellers peer out at the shining ribbon of asphalt that traces the Bow River valley west toward the continental divide.

Sheets of water pulse across the limestone faces of the Fairholme Range, Three Sisters Mountain and Mount Rundle. Gullies fill with runoff as sparse timberline forests and grassy slopes shed the rain their shallow soils cannot absorb. Cougar and Wind Creeks become brown and hungry. The Bow River rises and overflows its channels.

On days like this, the Bow River becomes virtually one with its surrounding landscape. The entire Bow watershed is running water, from the summits of cloud-enshrouded mountains to the rounded gravels of the river bed below. For just this brief time, running water makes tangible the complex web of living connections that bind the Bow River to the great surrounding mountain ecosystem.

Most people consider the Bow Glacier, on the Continental Divide north of Lake Louise, to be the source of the Bow River. Saying that the Bow begins in the Pacific Ocean, however, would be closer to truth.

The Pacific Ocean sprawls like an unfathomably vast humidifier between Asia and North America. The Earth's rotation on her axis sets winds in motion over the great expanse of sea. The winds sweep east and north across the blue Pacific, drawing immense masses of moisture-laden air up and across the continent where we live.

As air rises, it cools. Since warm air can hold more moisture than cold, rising air masses cool, cloud, and shed excess moisture as rain and snow.

Pulled by air ahead and pushed by air behind, the great Pacific weather systems drag bucketing sheets of rain across the British Columbia's Coast Mountains. Rolling eastward, the air masses again are forced to rise over the Selkirk and Purcell Mountains where they shed more moisture to grow giant cedars, devil's-club and grizzly bears.

Farther inland yet, towns like Cranbrook, Invermere and Golden bask in a balmy rain-shadow climate as the air masses continue to flood eastward. At length they bulge up against the widest, highest mountain mass of all — the Canadian Rockies.

The Bow River is born of the last of that Pacific Ocean moisture, wrung from the weather systems as they spill across the Continental Divide. Bow Glacier receives up to ten metres of snow each year, feeding meltwaters that drain to Bow Lake and thence into the newborn Bow River. The Pipestone River, Healy Creek, Spray River, Ghost and Kananaskis Rivers and countless smaller tributaries, each in turn, swell the Bow with its share of the Pacific Ocean's transported wealth.

Anglers fish for brown trout and mountain whitefish in the Bow near Exshaw. Paddlers ease their canoes through the river's riffles below Banff. Children bicycle along riverside trails at Lake Louise. All hear the chatter and murmur of the river. If they could understand its voices, they might hear tales about hidden places high in the Rockies where the headwaters rise, and rumours of the great global forces that sustain the river and its landscapes.

There was a time, only a few thousands of years ago, when

snow fell more heavily on the high country and melted more slowly. For millennia, immense glaciers filled the valleys of the Bow and its tributaries, flowing slowly eastward. Rivers of ice carved out the valleys that hold today's more modest river flows. The glaciers steepened valley walls, flattened the valley floors, and left behind complex landscape patterns when at last — about 12,000 years ago — they melted back. Their remnants survive today in cold, sheltered refuges high in the mountains of Banff National Park.

Free of ice at last, the Bow Corridor began to evolve into today's rich ecological mosaic. Plants and animals that had survived the frozen millennia west of the Rockies began to spread east through Kicking Horse, Vermilion and Kananaskis passes. Prairie vegetation crept west from refugia south of the ice. Northern wildlife appeared from the east.

Along the Bow Corridor, glacial terraces, limestone mountains, valley-bottom springs and a mild, low-elevation climate uncommon in the Rocky Mountains offered new opportunities for life. Plants and animals that had evolved separately, in very different regions, encountered one another in the raw new landscape. A unique ecological complex evolved.

Thousands of people now live in or visit the Bow Corridor, but few spend much time contemplating the origins of the river, its landscape, and the ecological complexity they sustain. We live in the present, for the most part, and plan for the future. Our focus is too often on development and change, rather than history and continuity.

Nonetheless, unravelling the rich and revealing ecology of the Bow Corridor is a valuable exercise in fascination and humility. One could argue that no human plans for the Bow Corridor can have any ecological or ethical validity unless they are founded upon a sombre consideration of the relationships, processes and living complexity that give the place its history, its vitality and its identity.

We Albertans are proud of our Chinooks — warm winds

that sweep down from the Rocky Mountains and turn the prairie winter into short-lived springtime. The Bow Corridor, from Banff all the way east beyond Calgary, is a funnel for those Chinook winds. The Chinook, in fact, is all that remains of those great Pacific weather systems that leave so much snow in the high country. Depleted of moisture and warmed by their sudden descent to low elevations, the winds repeatedly sweep winter snow from south and west exposures.

Their mild winter climate and balmy summers make low-elevation valleys and hillsides along the Bow Corridor exceptionally valuable. The cooler, heavily forested landscapes more typical of the Canadian Rockies sustain far less diversity and abundance of life. The montane ecoregion — as ecologists describe this landscape of mixed grassland, aspen thickets and forests of Douglas fir and lodgepole pine — exists in only a few other parts of Alberta.

Up to thirteen hundred elk spend each winter in the montane, avoiding the deep snows of the high country winter. Bighorn sheep, mule deer and other large animals also congregate on montane winter ranges. Here they can count on abundant grass, shallow snow and the occasional spell of mild weather.

Banff National Park's famous elk herds do not winter along the Bow Corridor by chance or coincidence. They are here because in all the cold, inhospitable northern Rockies, this is one place where they can generally be sure of surviving the winter.

The sunny south-facing benchlands above Canmore and the wind-blown ridges of Grotto and Pigeon mountains and Wind Ridge are vital to populations of elk, bighorn sheep and mule deer that range much farther afield each summer. If someone were to take away those winter ranges, a vast expanse of the southern Alberta Rockies would become ecologically impoverished.

Wolves and other large carnivores are just as dependent on the montane ecoregion and the Bow Corridor's windy ridges and slopes. Their fate is tied to that of the large grazing animals they eat. A rabies scare in the 1950s led the government to poison all the wolves south of Jasper National Park. It took until the late 1970s before single wolves and small packs reappeared in Banff National Park. They had spread southward from the still-wild northern forests of Alberta.

Today, wolves continue to colonize their ancestral ranges. Wolves from the Bow Valley have wandered as far south as Idaho and Wyoming. A major highway and railroad traverse the Bow Corridor, however, and the valley is subject to increasing development pressures. In all the Rocky Mountains, this narrow band of heavy traffic and human activity remains the most dangerous obstacle for large carnivores like the wolf. The single biggest killer of wolves in Banff National Park, according to wildlife biologist Paul Paquet, is the Trans-Canada Highway. As roads and development fragment montane valley bottoms, wolves and other large carnivores — small in number at the best of times — face ever-greater risk of death or disturbance.

Dr. Paquet has identified key movement corridors for wolves, cougars and bears that, so far, have helped these scarce animals avoid becoming separated into small, isolated populations. One such corridor extends from the Bow Valley through the Spray Lakes area into southern B.C. and Peter Lougheed Provincial Park. Another runs through the Wind Creek Valley/Skogan Pass area into Kananaskis Country. Both help wolves and other wildlife maintain essential genetic links between northern populations and those farther south.

For those who live in or visit the Bow Corridor, a chance sighting of a wolf loping along the Bow River floodplain, or a herd of elk grazing on the benchlands north of Canmore is something to savour and talk about. It is part of a unique quality of experience that this montane area offers. But it is also a reminder of the complex links that connect landscape, climate and wildlife populations within what Paul Paquet and other scientists call the Central

Rockies Ecosystem — an ecosystem whose heart is the Bow Corridor.

Ecosystems, of course, involve more than just the large animals. From the Cordilleran flycatcher to the brown thrasher, from bull trout to wolverine, and from limber pine to sparrow's egg orchid, the Bow Corridor is a rich mix of prairie, western, alpine and northern plants and animals. The most sensitive elements of the ecosystem are often the least-known.

Long-toed salamanders, for example, are among the few amphibians that can thrive in the Rockies. Even so, only the gentle climate of the montane ecoregion suits this dark little salamander. Even there, its lifestyle confines it to a few specialized habitats.

Salamanders venture out of their homes in the soil and rotting logs of aspen forests, willow thickets and other montane habitats each May. They follow their instincts overland, back to the ponds of their birth. There they mate, then lay their eggs in shallow water. The spring sun warms the eggs until tiny black larvae, like little tadpoles, hatch out.

Long-toed salamanders were once widespread, but many populations have fallen victim to the changes that the 20th century brought to the Bow Corridor. National park wardens and provincial fisheries officers unwittingly helped to exterminate some populations by stocking small lakes and ponds with trout. Long-toed salamander larvae are easy prey for these predators. Dr. Geoff Holroyd of the Canadian Wildlife Service points out that Pilot Pond, in Banff National Park, was once known as Lizard Lake because of its salamander population. Trout stocking eliminated them.

In other parts of the Bow Corridor, roads block salamander migration routes. Wetland filling and gravel quarrying have eliminated breeding ponds. Long-toed salamanders are invisible and unknown to most of the people whose activities have changed their ecosystems. Consequently, they now survive in only a few ponds and wetlands along the Bow Corridor. These few vulnerable populations still make their annual journeys each May, unaware of mounting development pressures and land-use changes that threaten their future.

Mountain landscapes contain a great deal of ecological complexity. Their rugged terrain produces complex interplays among slope aspect, sunshine, drainage and wind. South-facing slopes receive more sun and wind than those that face north. As a result, southern exposures often have dry grassland, aspen forest and open Douglas fir forests. Denser forests of pine and spruce clothe north-facing slopes. Down along the river, where spring floods rearrange the floodplain year after year, thickets of water-loving willows and red-osier dogwoods alternate with rich old forests of spruce and balsam poplar. Rushes, dryas and mountain fireweed cover newly exposed river flats.

Geoff Holroyd's studies of wildlife populations in Banff National Park showed that the montane ecoregion has by far the greatest density and diversity of wildlife in the Rockies. Alluvial fans — fan-shaped landforms where tributary streams enter the main Bow valley — are among the most important habitats because of their poplar forests, rich soils and available water. Unfortunately, they are also the most desirable for development. Most Banff National Park campgrounds and tourist lodges, not to mention the entire towns of Banff, Exshaw, most of Canmore and the Deadman's Flats service area, occupy montane alluvial fans.

Other ecologically important habitats include grassland areas, the floodplain of the Bow River and its tributaries, old-growth Douglas fir forests, and areas of calcium-rich springs.

Some early land-use changes actually increased the ecological diversity of the Bow Corridor. Introduced rhubarb and pasture grasses colonized the slack heaps that resulted from early coal mines. Road clearing brought new weeds and exotic plants, some of which proved palatable to elk and small rodents. Park wardens and provincial fisheries staff added new species of fish — rainbow, brown and brook trout — to rivers and streams.

With each change, however, the Bow Corridor became a little different from what it had been when the Peigan, Kootenai and Stoney people had it to themselves. The unprecedented arrival of roads, bulldozers, exotic weeds and mortgages abruptly interrupted the long, gradual evolution that had been taking place ever since the retreat of the glaciers.

A century later, the Bow Corridor's scenic beauty camouflages the degree to which incremental change has compromised its ecosystem. Wolves are rare, otters and fishers extinct, and even elk appear unable to rebuild their populations outside Banff National Park. Grizzly bears seldom roam the Bow River's floodplain and, Paul Paquet warns, could disappear within a decade or two. Long-toed salamanders survive in only a few ponds. Most ecologically significant areas in the Corridor — places like Wind Valley, the Canmore benchlands, Yamnuska and Grotto Mountain — now appear on the blueprints and plans of resort developers and mining companies.

"One of the penalties of an ecological education," American conservationist Aldo Leopold wrote half a century ago, "is that one lives alone in a world of wounds."

Human populations have mushroomed in the Bow Corridor over the past century; nobody can be said to live alone there now. Even so, few are conscious of the extent of the ecosystem's wounds.

Many of those wounds can, to some degree, be healed. Most are products of ignorance, inflicted by generations of Albertans whose optimism and ambitions exceeded their ecological knowledge. Understanding and knowledge, at least among a growing minority, has increased in recent years.

Ecological restoration — and the protection of the still-considerable ecological wealth that survives in the Bow Corridor and its surrounding mountain ecosystem — will not be easy. In part, they will depend on widespread knowledge of how the greater ecosystem works. They will also require a strong community commitment to sustaining the ecological diversity that makes the Bow Corridor so rich and unique a place.

Perhaps most important, the survival of the Bow Corridor's ecological integrity will require that thousands of human beings who now feel a personal stake in the Bow Corridor recognize that ecological principles apply to humans too. Just as the Bow ecosystem can never support more than a few hundred elk or a few dozen wolves, there is also a finite limit on how much human activity and development it can sustain. ❧ *(1994)*

Through a Grizzly's Eyes:
Ecosystem thinking in a fragmented world

IT IS LATE AFTERNOON. The sound of meltwater is everywhere. The dull thunder of avalanches fills the valley as mountains release winter-long accumulations of snow.

In the alders at the base of an avalanche slope a grizzly lies on his back, one paw poised above him and his head twisted to the side. He opens his eyes and focuses on the branches above him, then closes them again and heaves a phlegmy sigh. A fox sparrow bursts into song nearby.

Below, the rushing of Sage Creek mingles with the muted sound of wind in pines. The air is hazy with humidity and soft with spring.

The bear dozes. The long day fades.

As the first evening breeze comes sliding down the gullies, bringing a fresh chill from timberline snowfields, the bear stands and shakes himself. He tests the air, then follows his nose to a newly exposed patch of brown vegetation. Uprooting a clump of sweet vetch with one swipe of his claws, he munches on the stringy roots.

In the forest, varied thrushes are singing.

A bullet strikes the ground by his face. The grizzly sits back on his haunches, shocked. The rifle's crack echoes down the valley.

Another bullet strikes, this time behind the bear.

He lumbers for the timber, head weaving as he tries to find a scent that will tell him what is going on.

The third bullet creases the big bear's hump just as human scent hits his nostrils. Like a ball of silver-tipped fur, the grizzly races into the trees as one last bullet ricochets into the alders.

Behind him, the hunters are left with the dilemma of deciding what to do next. They have driven by four-wheel-drive truck to the end of a logging road, through vast clearcuts, to hunt grizzlies legally during British Columbia's spring bear season in hunting zone 4-1. They know how scarce grizzlies are, especially one as big as this. One hunter is sure his shot hit the bear. But it is growing dark. Neither of them wishes to surprise a wounded grizzly at close range.

The grizzly, however, is half a kilometre away, moving steadily up the valley. The memory of the gunshots is fading as his powerful nose filters countless familiar odours from the mountain night — resin, snowmelt, mold, new buds.

By morning, the grizzly has crossed the continental divide, into the high country at the headwaters of the Waterton River. Wind roars through timberline firs as the bear descends to a small creek.

He forages halfheartedly along the stream meadow, but the ground is well frozen at this elevation. Wandering into a patch of old-growth spruce trees, he beds down against a log. He tries to lick the sore spot on his shoulder, but his head will not twist that far. Eventually he stretches out on his side, sighs, and falls asleep.

It is unlikely that bears let worries disturb their sleep; in any case, he need not worry tonight. Although he is still in the same great mountain ecosystem, well within his normal home range, he has crossed an invisible line in the darkness.

Two hours ago he could be legally shot and killed as a game animal. Now, he sleeps in a national park, protected by law.

For three days the grizzly works his way downstream. The wind on this side of the Rockies seems to howl endlessly, sweeping its thawing breath down from spindrift-topped peaks into the brown foothills.

Digging roots one night along the edge of Blakiston Creek, still in Waterton Lakes National Park, the bear's hackles lift. He freezes, nose working, small eyes flickering. The wind has brought the scent of bear cubs.

He moves forward, pigeon-toed and stiff-legged. Something moves at the edge of the grassland. A low rumble rises in his throat.

A loud woof answers him.

The female charges from a clump of silverberry, snarling and swinging her paws. She stops a few steps short of the big male, moaning and drooling. Her ears are laid back. She clacks her jaws ominously.

Behind her, three cubs flee, hesitate, and dash back to cower behind their mother.

The male lowers his head as if to smell something in the grass, and walks a few paces to one side, his nostrils full of cub smell and his small brain full of blood. Still, the female's desperate rage makes him cautious. The female makes another rush and he braces for the attack, but again she turns aside. This time she herds her cubs away. The male does not follow.

Female grizzlies defend their cubs very aggressively, partly because male grizzlies kill cubs. Since grizzlies are not inclined to climb trees as black bears are, grizzly mothers do not have the option of sending their cubs up a tree for safety. Instead, they sometimes find themselves forced to attack other bears to protect their young.

In Glacier and Waterton Lakes National Parks, grizzlies are safe from hunters. They are not, however, safe from the growing numbers of people who visit the parks to savour the scenery and tramp the trails. The aggressive instincts of female grizzlies are a constant hazard, because female grizzlies react to hikers very much like they do to other bears. As more people crowd into bear country, attacks by grizzlies on humans become inevitable. Human injuries usually result in dead bears.

The grizzly swims the Waterton River. The farther he travels east, the better the forage. The high passes are still locked in winter but here at lower elevations, where Chinook winds sweep away much of the winter snow, green grass and new spring flowers are everywhere. The grizzly lost almost a quarter of his body weight during his winter sleep, so the new vegetation on his spring range is like ambrosia.

Several days later he crosses another invisible boundary onto the Blood Indian Reserve, skirting a gas well. He leaves a string of huge, pigeon-toed tracks along the muddy well road. Then, completely unaware of it, he crosses back into the national park. One end of the glacier lily patch was Indian land. By the time he ate the last lily bulb, he was in the park. They all tasted the same.

Late in June, the bear is in Poll Haven Community Pasture, well to the east of where he spent the winter. Rain mists the aspen forests and meadows. In the fogged treetops above Lee Creek, a robin sings steadily into the sodden dusk. This piece of the Crown is owned — a human notion, alien to grizzlies and all other living things — by the Alberta government.

Green odours are everywhere. The bear steps over fallen logs and through rain-drenched buffaloberry shrubs, oblivious to the wet as he follows his nose from one wet green smell to the next. He has been gaining weight steadily these past few weeks.

He is moving crosswinds when a delightful smell hits him square in the nostrils: the rich, strong odour of rotting flesh.

The cow, bloated and swollen, sprawls where lightning killed it a week ago. It is a windfall to the bear, who normally eats only vegetation.

Two days later, the cow carcass is nearly gone. The ravens who argue all day long in the treetops have splattered the remaining tatters of hide and broken bones with their droppings. Three coyotes have been working on the carcass too, carrying away bits and pieces whenever the bear's back was turned.

As he emerges from the timber for one last meal, the grizzly detects a new odour, that of engine oil and exhaust. New tire tracks mar the trampled ground near the carcass.

Poll Haven used to be part of Waterton Lakes National Park. The federal government surrendered it to Alberta in 1947 so that local ranchers could pasture their cattle there. Unfortunately, it is also an important spring range for grizzly bears. When range cattle die, bears scavenge on the carcasses. Rarely, a bear learns to kill cows.

When bears eat domestic cattle, provincial authorities remove the bears. Sometimes this means trapping the bear and removing it far from the Crown. In other cases it means killing it. Either way, the ecosystem loses a bear. In 1986 and 1987 alone, Alberta Fish and Wildlife removed ten grizzlies from Poll Haven to protect domestic cows.

When the Fish and Wildlife truck returns pulling a bear trap the following afternoon, however, the grizzly is already several kilometres away. He is bedded just below a ridge top in northern

Montana, fast asleep.

He is safe now. In the United States of America, the same bear that hunters can legally kill in B.C. dodges hikers and cameras in Waterton Lakes National Park, and is considered an agricultural pest in Alberta grazing lands, receives the full protection of the U.S. Endangered Species Act. It is a criminal offense for humans to disturb the bear on this side of yet another invisible line.

None of this would make sense to the bear, if he were aware of it. This is all his home range, all the same ecosystem. As the seasons change he will inevitably cross those invisible lines again and again. Each time he crosses another jurisdictional boundary, he encounters different hazards, land-use patterns and human philosophies.

This October, when a poacher kills him beside a gas-well road in Alberta's Bow-Crow Forest Reserve, the grizzly will have become another victim of ecosystem fragmentation.

The Crown of the Continent Ecosystem — where the Rocky Mountains give way to the great central plains of North America — is a spectacular tapestry of bunchgrass prairie, aspen forest, evergreens, castellated mountains, and wind. Viewed from outer space, it forms a pattern clearly distinct from the surrounding landscapes. Mountains fill the centre, prairie rims the edges, and forested valleys send their waters to three oceans.

To the west, headwater valleys feed the Columbia River system, flowing at length to the Pacific Ocean. To the north, streams drain to the Oldman River and thence by way of the Saskatchewan River to Hudson's Bay. To the east, other streams hasten to join the Missouri and, at length, the Gulf of Mexico.

The watersheds of the Crown may drain to different oceans, but they share geological origins, landscape patterns, weather systems, and wildlife populations.

From outer space, large patterns are more visible than fine

details. From an orbiting satellite, for example, one can easily see great Pacific weather systems rolling inland across the continent to squeeze up against the chilly heights of the Crown's 2,000-metre mountains. As clouds form and thicken, those weather systems shed rain and snow along the western reaches of the Crown. To the east, where mountains give way to prairie, the descending winds — drier and warmer now — sweep across aspen thickets and fescue grassland.

Those sorts of patterns are visible from outer space. The intricate details of bunchgrass prairie, with its dozens of species of native plants, are not. The gas well roads that trace a spider web pattern across the corners of the Crown barely show on satellite photographs. Cattle, dotting the checkerboard grain and hay fields along the edge of the Crown are even more difficult to detect.

Other manmade changes, however, are clearly visible. On the British Columbia side, vast clearcuts look like mange on the Crown's green face. Highways slice into Crowsnest Pass and Waterton Lakes and Glacier National Parks. Irrigation reservoirs sparkle in the sun along the eastern edge.

Down on earth, wholeness disappears into detail. It is hard to see an ecosystem from the perspective of the average human being, or bear. Mountains block the view. One literally cannot see the forest for the trees. Day-to-day detail proscribes the lives, and imaginations, of people who live in Pincher Creek, Polebridge, St. Mary, the Blackfeet Reservation, or any of the Crown's many ranches.

Our ground-level view of Earth may explain why, today, Waterton Lakes National Park seems more real than the Crown of the Continent ecosystem — though we invented the park and the ecosystem already existed. The Canada-U.S. border slices blindly across drainage divides and wildlife winter ranges, yet most consider this artificial line more meaningful than the watersheds it severs.

Humans invent boundaries, and then are forever confined by them. It seems ironic that some lines that now confound efforts to sustain the Crown of the Continent were originally drawn to protect it.

George Bird Grinnell, an American hunter and adventurer, visited the Crown in the late 1800s. Grinnell was impressed by the area's red and green mountains, crystal streams and abundant wildlife. Its unusual three-way continental watershed divide fascinated him. Grinnell ardently promoted the idea of a park that would protect this spectacular area from logging and development. Even in the late 1800s, he warned, frontier ambitions threatened its biological diversity.

"The game is almost all gone now from mountain and plain," he wrote. "Buffalo and bison are extinct everywhere, but in the dense forest a few moose, elk and deer still exist and, as of old, bears prowl through the timber...."

Almost a century later, the threatened grizzly bear still prowls the timber. Thanks to Grinnell and Canadian rancher-conservationist Frederick Godsal, both the U.S. and Canadian governments established parks early in this century to protect part of the Crown. Glacier National Park, in northern Montana, and Waterton Lakes National Park, in southwestern Alberta, together enclose more than 4,625 km^2 of the Crown of the Continent Ecosystem.

This is still too small by grizzly bear standards. An adult male's home range may cover more than a thousand square kilometres. Grizzlies survive today mostly because of the abundant wildlife habitat outside the parks, in B.C.'s Kishinena drainage, Alberta's South Castle and Mill Creek watersheds and U.S. Forest Service lands in Montana. All remained wild and remote for most of this century.

That is no longer the case. On Alberta provincial lands, roads and pipelines invaded the wilderness as large petroleum companies developed the Crown's rich natural gas fields. The new access continues to open the area to hunting pressure and off-road vehicle use. Logging companies, too, created new access — and far more extensive habitat change — in both Alberta and B.C. National parks concentrated roads and tourist facilities in the most productive valley-bottom areas. Developers continue to promote ski hills, golf courses and even water slide parks in other valleys. Elk, bears and wolves are agricultural pests to some of the Crown's ranchers.

To animals, the Crown of the Continent is a whole — one great, interconnected living system. Wildlife continue to live according to their ancient patterns but humans are changing their ecosystem at an accelerating rate. So far, we humans have had difficulty being sensitive to one another's needs, not to mention the needs of the ecosystem as a whole.

Is there a future for wide-ranging wildlife like the grizzly bear in southwestern Alberta? If there is not, then is there any real future for the ecosystem? And as the ecosystem erodes, what kind of future is there for the human beings who now share this special place?

We are the latest comers to the Crown, but we risk changing it forever before we have really begun to understand it. As we change our environment, we change ourselves; just as the bear is ultimately defined by the ecosystem of which he is an element, so are we.

The past century has seen repeated battles over who will get what share of the Crown's jewels. Only now are we beginning to step outside those selfish arguments and ask how we can live together here without destroying the things that keep this ecosystem whole and — in the final analysis — make us whole, too. ❧

(1991)

Under the Arch: The Foothills

The Curse of the Cow

IT ISN'T THAT I DISLIKE COWS. Then again, I couldn't honestly say that I count any cows among my closest friends. One thing I must confess, however, in the interests of full disclosure, is that I enjoy few things more than a good t-bone steak. From a cow.

So I can't agree with k.d. lang's now-famous line: "Beef stinks." Beef's great; cows stink.

I grew up in western Alberta. I learned early what it feels like to step in a cowpie. Fresh cowpies have no redeeming virtues. The older ones that have developed a good crust on top are better. I like to step on them and watch the gooey stuff come out the cracks. Over the years I've left boot prints in a lot of cowpies along a lot of Alberta trout streams.

Give me the smell of a cowpie, or the sight of a churned-up floodplain, and I think of fishing. That, in a way, is the whole point. For years I never even thought of objecting to the fact that every trout stream in western Alberta is full of cows. I guess I just assumed that this was how God created them.

It is not. Cows, and their leavings are graphic examples of what happens when humans try to improve on Nature.

The truth is, cows wreck streams. Cows wreck forests. Cows wreck grasslands. Cows can even wreck your arteries, if you let them. Now some people are saying that cows wreck the atmosphere. It isn't the bomb, apparently, that is going to end human civilization; it's the Holstein.

Actually, that's an awfully heavy burden of responsibility to lay on a harmless genetic clone with barely any brain at all. It's not as if a cow can form the intent to do harm. Let's back up here a minute: it isn't poor old Mrs. Wiggins that's at fault. It's you and I. Because we eat beef. And that means someone, somewhere, is raising a cow to provide us with it.

I don't hate cows. I hate seeing cows. I hate smelling cows. I hate what they do to my habitat. But who could hate a cow? They have such nice eyes, no matter what the other end might look like. Cows, as much as the landscapes they wreck, are innocent victims of human arrogance.

When it comes to cows, I share the late Edward Abbey's poetic sentiments, expressed in a letter to the *High Country News*:

> *Oh give me a home*
> *where the buffalo roam*
> *and the elk and the antelope play;*
> *where seldom is seen*
> *the hamburger machine*
> *and the flies are not swarming all day.*

The domestic cow is not native to North America. In fact, most of the planet's 1.4 billion cows are foreign to the places they wreck. The cow originated as a species of wild kine that frequented southern Asia's swamps and river bottoms. Through generations of selective breeding, it has devolved into a bewildering variety of meat and milk machines. The cow is history's answer to whether evolution is best left in God's hands or taken over by humans. Nature would never have created the awkward, pink-eyed, dung-encrusted, meaty dunderheads to which we have reduced southern Asia's wild cattle.

While cows now come in a variety of breeds, shapes and sizes, certain traits still breed true. For example, cows cannot resist wet places. This accounts for the cowpies along my trout streams. It also explains why finding a spring or seep on most of western Canada's low-elevation public lands that cows haven't overgrazed and trampled is virtually impossible. Trout

Unlimited, an angler's organization based mostly in Alberta, Ontario and B.C., spends nearly all of its donated funds and volunteer time restoring trout streams damaged by cattle.

Cattle congregating near springs and streams not only trample fragile vegetation and ruin stream banks; they also contaminate drinking water with their droppings. A graduate student studying cows in one Ontario watershed found that each animal stepped into a stream on average 2.5 times per day. While in the stream, there was a 20 percent probability that the cow would defecate. This suggests two things: they hand out graduate degrees for some very obscure stuff, and the beaver (which, unlike cows and beefeaters, is native to Canada) has gotten a bum rap for the spread of parasites like Giardia.

Normal range management practice aims at having cows consume about 50 percent of available native grass cover each year, leaving the stubble to hold the soil down. However, sustained grazing at this intensity — besides leaving native elk, voles and other grazers with a much-reduced standard of living — leads to soil erosion and cuts the grassland's ability to trap snow and rain and absorb water. The result: diminished native wildlife populations, soil erosion, flash floods and depleted watercourses.

Many streams that once flowed year-round now dry up in summer because of the impact of cattle on their watersheds. This is not good for fish. It is also not good for the rest of the aquatic ecosystem, nor for people who value, and depend on, healthy landscapes.

In western Canada, irrigation farmers often make matters worse by sucking water from streams in midsummer to irrigate alfalfa, corn and hay — crops they then feed to those same cattle. Alberta, which has more than two thirds of all Canada's irrigated crop acreage, uses almost as much irrigation water to produce food for cows as it does to produce food for humans.

Water-guzzling crops like alfalfa thrive on the super-subsidized water of southern Alberta irrigation country; virtually the entire Alberta feedlot industry is now situated there as a result.

The equation, then, is as follows: prairie rivers, already suffering from overgrazed watersheds, are sucked nearly dry to water fields of alfalfa and feed grains. These crops are then fed to cows in crowded, smelly feedlots. Their excrement then oozes back into the watercourses, finding its way at length to the shrunken river where its decomposition creates an oxygen deficit. Meanwhile, cattle graze and trample the sickened river's floodplain. Little wonder that the World Wildlife Fund considers prairie river bottoms to be among the world's most endangered ecosystems.

Still, Canadians like beef; the average Canadian eats close to his or her own weight in beef each year. Beef is big business. So more feedlots demand more cheap feed; more farmers demand more cheap irrigation water; and governments cheerfully borrow more money to build more dams on more rivers and streams — dams like the Rafferty and the Oldman.

Last year I went to a benefit concert at Calgary's Silver Dollar Action Centre. Ian Tyson and Michael Martin Murphy had organized it to raise funds to fight two dams — Alberta's notorious Oldman River Dam and the Two Forks Dam in the U.S.

The place was awash with cowboy hats, blue jeans and string ties. The cowboy music was great; so was the dinner that came with it. "I'm not gonna say anything about k.d. lang," shouted the Master of Ceremonies to a chorus of hoots and yells, "but I want you all to know that tonight we're eating good Alberta beef!"

Cowboys and pseudo cowboys alike cheered and dug in. Yet the dams we were there to fight were being built largely in response to a demand for the beef we so proudly consumed.

Cowboys raise less than 10 percent of Canada's cows on the open range today. The romantic West is gone; beef production today is just another kind of farming.

Nothing about this paradox is unique; few realize the diversity of often-subtle ways in which our appetite for beef degrades the world's ecosystems. Only recently has the popular media picked up on some of the most direct impacts — for example, the clearing of tropical rainforests to create pastures for American hamburger chains — or the more exotic impacts — for example, the fact that cows produce more than 500 billion litres of methane worldwide each year, contributing in their own small way to global warming.

However, there are many less obvious impacts. Few realize that one of Canada's greatest rivers, the Athabasca, is regularly treated with toxic chemicals to kill blackflies that harass cows. If no cows occupied Alberta's boreal fringe, the poisoning of the Athabasca could be left to pulp mills.

Farther north in Canada's boreal forest, some of the most heavily subsidized cattle operations in the world are moving closer to Wood Buffalo National Park. When agriculture officials became concerned that these cattle might catch brucellosis from native bison, they came up with a modest proposition. They instructed Parks Canada to wipe out every one of the four thousand or so bison occupying the boreal wilderness. The demand for cheap beef may yet lead to one of the greatest ecological holocausts in Canada's history. Where did those bison get their brucellosis in the first place? From cows, of course.

Cows eat grass, but ranches eat habitat. The spread of cattle into northern Canada's boreal forests has been going on for many years, but recently the public has begun to awaken to the environmental costs. In 1988, more than 500 people turned out at a public meeting in Glendon, Alberta to protest government clearing of forests near Lac La Biche for livestock grazing. Ray Makowecki, Regional Director of the Alberta Fish and Wildlife Division, said at the time: "What is happening in the East Frenchman Lake area has been happening in the last twenty years in all fringe areas with agriculture. It's marginal farmland, but also the best wildlife habitat we have left."

Cows can wipe out wildlife in more subtle ways, too. Kootenay National Park, for example, has cow problems without having cows. Traffic on the Banff-Windermere Parkway kills up to 100 animals, mostly elk, each year. Some of these are hit by trucks laden with magnesite ore that is mined south of the park and hauled north to be processed in Alberta. Magnesite makes, among other things, a product that helps feedlot cattle produce more meat from less forage. Although this is one place in western Canada where elk do not have to compete with cows for food, some elk lose to them anyway!

In the United States, a growing movement calls for the elimination of "range maggots" from public lands. Conservationists say that the land will produce more economic benefits if it is left to recover from the damage caused by livestock. Their battle cry, "Livestock free by '93!" comes not from concerns over esoteric connections among magnesite mines, cows and elk, but from the simple fact that cows can destroy native vegetation not adapted to bovine gastronomy.

Cows are not discriminating eaters, and most native vegetation cannot cope with continual heavy cropping by high-tech water buffalos. The upshot: range experts consider an estimated 10 percent of the American West to be in a state of desertification due to overgrazing. A U.S. Senate study found that more than three quarters of Bureau of Land Management rangeland was in poor to fair condition. In the Kamloops and Okanagan areas of B.C. extremely destructive weeds like spotted knapweed and cheatgrass have virtually taken over entire landscapes; overgrazing by cattle suppressed native bunchgrasses and created open soil niches for exotic weeds to invade.

Canada's prairie provinces and the Alberta foothills, both of which fed millions of bison and elk before the coming of the cow, are better off. Nonetheless, cattle severely degrade many forested rangelands in both Alberta and B.C., especially near watercourses. In Alberta's forest reserves, according to biologist Lorne Fitch, cattle overgrazing is a two-headed monster.

"On the one hand," he says, "we have done such a good job of controlling forest fires that in some traditional grazing areas forest expansion is decreasing the forage available."

The fact that today's cows are a lot bigger than the ones that were used to calculate stocking rates compounds the problem of shrinking natural rangelands. "An Animal Unit Month (AUM) is supposed to represent one cow and calf unit," says Fitch. "If an area has a capacity of twenty AUMs, then it should have enough forage to support twenty cows and calves for one month."

Since livestock producers have bred today's cattle to be much heavier, however, they also eat a lot more forage. That piece of rangeland, even if spreading forests have not shrunken it, may produce only enough grass to feed ten or fifteen of today's mega-cows. Nevertheless, the rancher is still pasturing twenty. In the fall, when ranchers pull cows off their forest ranges and elk move down to winter on their traditional meadows, not much remains. When starving elk try to feed on ranchers' haystacks, the government responds with yet another cow subsidy: "nuisance" animal control programs aimed at native elk. Then, when hungry wolves turn up wondering where all the prey went, the taxpayer pays to poison them, too.

"When I think of the massive damage done to our public lands by cattle and other domestics, I can begin to understand the growing movement to ban domestic grazing on public lands," said Alberta Fish and Game Association President Dr. Niels Damgaard in a 1989 letter to the *Alberta Farmer's Advocate*. "The destruction of nesting habitat, stream bank damage, destruction of thermal cover, all done by grazing cattle are but a few examples. I'm sorry, but I cannot thank our grazing lease holders for perpetuating this destruction. A draft report on Fish and Wildlife prepared for the Alberta Conservation Strategy clearly identified cattle as the major reason for habitat destruction in Southern Alberta...."

If the common cow has so few redeeming qualities, then, what are we to do?

Some folks have already gone vegetarian. Don't eat cows; eat what cows eat. Canadian Cattlemen's Association spokesperson Dennis Laycraft, however, coyly points out that vegetarians produce methane too. His organization has recently launched an all-out public relations campaign to improve beef's image. In these difficult times, some members of the Cattle Commission give the word "vegetarian" the same inflection that used to be reserved for "communist."

If you don't fancy a life of lentils and kidney beans, then you might try switching to other meats, like chicken. It takes 2 pounds of grain to produce 1 pound of chicken meat, while it takes 7 pounds of grain to produce a pound of feedlot beef. At least your protein will not cost the environment quite as much.

I try to feed my family elk and deer. It is leaner and healthier than beef, and produced by free, happy animals who have never known the sounds and smells of a feedlot or slaughterhouse. Wild elk and deer make more efficient use of forage than cows, and cause far less environmental damage. Besides, I like to be around elk and deer, and their habitat, a lot more than I like to be around cows and what they do to habitat. As long as people want more beef, there will be less room for elk

— not to mention wolves and grizzlies. Conversely, the more people demand elk and deer, the more demand there will be for wild, natural landscapes.

However, think of all twenty-six million of us Canadians wandering around the landscape each fall with rifles, shotguns, bows and spears. This may not be the most practical solution to the curse of the cow. It might, on the other hand, help significantly with human overpopulation which is, after all, at the root of the problem.

Whatever your choice, however, the bottom line is this: eat less beef. Eat a lot less beef.

Few Canadians, so far, have adopted the "Livestock Free by '93" battle cry of our neighbours to the south. After all, many cattle operations are well managed, sustain local economies and contribute to habitat diversity. Ranchers are human beings. Most care deeply about the health of the land that sustains them. It is possible to fence cows away from streams and springs, move them off sensitive vegetation, and protect them from pests and disease in ways that don't decimate ecosystems.

These things are possible. But we humans, like cows, tend to be lazy, unimaginative and tradition-bound. In too many cases these things are not done.

I grew up with cowpies; Canada grew up on beef. It looks like cows are here to stay. After all, language and geography may divide us, but one thing binds this nation from coast to coast: we eat cows. Maybe trampled floodplains, polluted streams, overgrazed watersheds, poisoned predators, slaughtered bison, barbed wire and irrigation dams are a small price to pay for national unity.

On the other hand that sounds like every other place in the world where the domestic cow has reduced unique ecosystems to the lowest common denominator of degraded landscape. Mr. Spicer, sir, my vision of a Canada worth standing on guard for has a whole lot fewer cows. Instead, it includes more wild elk, native grasslands, healthy streams, free-ranging predators and unfenced wilderness. Would you put that in your report, sir? *(1991)*

In Praise of Cows

IN MEDICINE HAT, Alberta, not too long ago, the Southern Alberta Grazing Association invited rancher Sherm Ewing to talk about cows and the environment.

Notwithstanding all the abuse the ranching industry has received lately from "...starry-eyed enviro-cranks who are usually college-trained idiots," Ewing said, "I think we've done a pretty good job of taking care of the environment over the years and we've used some common sense. The message I've got for you is that when cattle can be used for the benefit of the environment, make a lot of noise about it."

As someone who has taken his own share of potshots at the common grass-burner myself, my ears are a little hot. I also have a college education, and the longer I am involved in conservation advocacy, the more I find myself waking up in the morning feeling like an enviro-crank. Maybe if the environment won with some kind of frequency I would start feeling differently. Whatever my excuse, his comments struck a little close to home. Is my distaste for living cows unfounded?

To be fair, let us reexamine those sway-backed, bland-eyed meat machines that crop Canada's wildlife ranges from coast to coast. Have they any redeeming virtues, or are we enviro-cranks right?

They have. I cannot tell a lie. The cow is still better than the real estate speculator, bulldozer or multinational coal company. Where cows roam, there is still room for nature. Elsewhere, there often is not.

In fact, if it were not for the beef industry, hunters, anglers and naturalists would find themselves confined to a lot less habitat than they now enjoy, a century after the first real estate broker arrived in the West.

Native grasslands from the Alberta foothills east to Manitoba's tall-grass prairie evolved for millennia under the constant influence of grazing animals. Millions of elk, bison, pronghorns and mule deer ranged the native grasslands. Historians estimate that sixty million buffalo roamed the Great Plains in 1800. By 1850, there were only half as many. The plains bison was virtually extinct by the end of the 19th century; fewer than fifty survived in the world.

The ranchers who came to western Canada in the late 1870s and early 1880s did not see their role as restoring grazing animals to a depleted ecosystem. Nevertheless, that is what they did. The animal that they brought had different habits than the native bison — cows love wetlands, while bison prefer to range across the uplands — but they ate grass and forbs. The prairie ecosystem needed them.

One of the best things the ranchers did — although motivated, again, by self-interest more than concern for the public good — was to lobby the government to keep sodbusters out of the West. Overgrazing can make grassland sick but ploughing it up to grow crops kills it. An overgrazed native pasture contains forty to sixty species of native plants and can still produce longspurs, grouse, voles and other native animals. A ploughed field contains maybe five to ten exotic plants and very few animals.

Today, the most diverse native landscapes in the prairie

region are those where ranching has continued to keep the plough at bay. The rich mixed-grass prairie of Alberta's Milk River country and Saskatchewan's Frenchman River watershed, the fescue grasslands of Alberta's Rumsey Block, Porcupine Hills and foothills, and the wheatgrass ranges of B.C.'s Chilcotin and Nicola valleys are among the richest wildlife ranges in the West.

Those who value native wildlife probably have more to gain by forming alliances with the cattle industry to promote continued cattle production on native ranges than by fighting to free the range of cows.

All the same, cows have unquestionably wrecked much of the West. From an ecological point of view, there can be good cattle management, and there can be bad cattle management. In too many areas, the bad prevails.

Stimson Creek, in southwestern Alberta, is a muddied, eroded remnant of the trout stream it once was. The foothills grazing allotments of Alberta's Bow-Crow forest are full of weeds that got established through overgrazing and trampling by cows. Cattle continue to trample and foul nearly every spring and creek bottom in southern Alberta and B.C.

Bad cattle management can be reversed, however. In many cases, the pressure to manage cattle better has come from the range industry itself, rather than from environmentalists who too often limit ourselves to demanding that the cows go.

Lorne Fitch, Regional Biologist for the Alberta Fish and Wildlife Division's southern region, told me about one rancher who decided to restore a wounded valley on his own. Hilton Pharis runs cattle on a little piece of God's country, near the head of Todd Creek.

"He told me one day that he felt bad about some of the changes he had seen on his land during his lifetime," said

Lorne. "He said that there used to be a lot more grass and brush along the creek when he was a kid. He said that before he died he wanted to do something that would leave the place better than he found it."

With several of his neighbours, Mr. Pharis sought advice from Lorne and his staff. Then he went to work fencing the stream banks and spring seeps along Todd Creek. Once he had recognized the problems his cattle had created, he rolled up his sleeves and went to work to solve them. Today the creek is clean and sweet again. Trout abound. Willows and other riparian plants have rebounded. Cows still graze the stream bottom, too — but only for a brief period each year when the grass and stream banks are most resistant to damage.

If the West had no range industry, we would also have a lot less native prairie, and a lot less wildlife habitat. Sadly, we are part of a society that abhors an economic vacuum. If you can't raise beef on a patch of land, someone is going to have to plough it, pave it, or build a summer home on it. Heck, you can't just leave it sitting there.

In retrospect, Sherm Ewing is mostly right. I would far rather meet a cow in my trout stream than see the last bits of wild prairie ploughed up for wheat, the foothills scraped to their bones by the coal industry, or rural subdivisions carpeting what used to be wild rangeland.

The most vital challenge for hunters and anglers is not to get the cows out of the country, nor even to get those offensive "No Trespassing" signs off the fenceposts at the corners of some public land grazing leases. The highest priority for the future may be for conservationists to forge strong, cooperative relations with the range cattle industry. The late twentieth century is not a good time to stand divided against the myriad forces that continue to threaten public lands, wildlife habitat, and the wide-open spaces we all love and value. ❧ *(1993)*

Unicorns in the Whaleback

YOU CAN ALWAYS GO BACK to the Whaleback and it will be there.

In a world where favourite places and secret retreats vanish almost overnight, that is reassuring.

It changes, of course. In spring, you might arrive to find the slopes suddenly green, crowned with brilliant gold where giant, sunflower-like blooms of balsamroot have suddenly exploded from places where snowdrifts lay only a month ago. Later, in the brilliant glare of the midsummer sun, the balsamroot may be faded, its time past. Instead, the hills may glisten with a strange reflective gold where a billion rough fescue seed heads are ripening in the heat.

The gold of ripening bunchgrass lasts only a week or two, then fades to the familiar brown of foothills Alberta. The first howling Chinooks of winter arrive soon after to try to bow down the Whaleback's stunted forests of limber pines and Douglas firs. But those trees have spent their whole lives bracing against the wind, their roots down in the cracks of the lichen-crusted sandstone outcrops that crown the long ridges. They are ancient trees, some of them, and the progeny of even more ancient trees that came before. They belong here, and so they dance and seethe untroubled in the wild winds that roar down off the Livingstone Range winter after winter.

Elk bed all day beneath those dancing branches, then feed by moonlight on wind-bared grasslands.

The Whaleback changes through the seasons, but doesn't change in the big ways to which my generation has grown accustomed. I went looking for a favourite deer hunting forest one fall and it was gone completely: every trail, every chickadee, every remembered corner. Alfalfa, newly-seeded,

110

sprouted from the ground where it once had stood.

You can always go back to the Whaleback, even if you may never be able to go back to other places again.

This spring I went back, uncertain in my own mind why I was doing so. Sometimes, when you know you can always go back, you put off visiting until far too much time has passed. I did that with my father, and now he is gone. That had something to do with my decision to return.

This past spring, Amoco applied to the Alberta government for permission to drill for natural gas there. Suddenly the unimaginable had become possible: the Whaleback might soon fall prey to the twentieth-century epidemic of roads, gas wells, and industrial noise. I realized that even the Whaleback might not survive forever — at least, not as the wild, secluded and inestimably rich place that it has always been.

My children never knew their maternal grandmother and barely knew their paternal grandfather before he died. They bear their genes and their names, but those people who formed a vital part of their heritage are gone. They are certain to be the poorer for having missed the chance to know them. At least Gail and I could make sure they knew the Whaleback before it, too, could be taken from them.

So Gail and I brought the kids with us.

Shooting stars were blooming in their millions, tucked down among matted tussocks of last year's bunchgrass. The sun was warm and the breeze gentle, rich with the green odours of new aspen leaves and melting snow banks. We turned our faces to the roadless north, and the kids raced ahead into the Whaleback.

Bluebirds flitted around us as we followed the brown swell of the main ridge up from the Oldman valley. Winter-weary legs struggled against gravity, and Katie and Brian started to make rebellious noises as their parents led them steadily uphill. At length we clambered out onto an outcropping of sandstone, crusted with orange, black and gray lichens, like the ancient bones of the earth. Below lay a mosaic of aspen, willow, fescue grassland and fir forests — the rich ecological mosaic that typifies what remains of Alberta's tiny montane ecoregion.

The kids drank lemonade. We looked north and west into a landscape unmarred by roads, development or air pollution.

I once climbed the same ridge in the darkness of an early November morning. I will always remember the shadowed landscape going on and on into the north without a single light to break the darkness of the hills. Even so, the pale hills reflected the glow of the blazing millions of stars that studded the blue-black band of sky that stretched below the chinook arch.

The anxious bellowing of a cow in the valley below reminded us that the Whaleback country, though it has survived the industrial juggernaut of the 20th century, nonetheless sustains human economy. We could see no cows, however; only a small band of mule deer retreating into the dark forest two ridges over and a kilometre away.

I'm a father; I wanted to find some way to impress the kids with the significance of this hike and this place. Fathers feel obliged to pontificate about that sort of thing.

The kids, however, were too busy pretending to be lost in the wilderness. Their voices piped happily in the clear spring air as they clambered among the ancient rocks and tried to climb the gnarled old limber pines.

Once Katie ran to me and said, urgently, "Daddy, is this the kind of place where unicorns could live?"

"Yes," I said, "although I think they don't like to be around grownups."

112

"Good," she said, and hurried back to the others.

I was right, too. Creatures of myth and exceptional beauty would be more likely to survive in the Whaleback than in the other crowded landscapes to which we have reduced so much of Alberta. Later that day as we picked our wind-burned way out of the Whaleback wildland, the kids said nothing about having seen any.

Corey did, however, point out a golden eagle.

It traced long arcs as it rose on the spring breeze out of Bob Creek Valley. It knew, like us, that you can always come back to the Whaleback. No doubt it had been doing so for many years.

Its offspring, I pray, will still ride the air currents over the same montane mosaic when Gail's and my kids come back, years from now, with their own kids. There will still be mule deer, cattle and bluebirds. The chinook wind will still make pine trees dance, and the nights, if they should choose to wait and see, will still be dark.

My grandchildren will gaze into the distance — because in the Whaleback there will still be distance — hoping, perhaps, to spot a unicorn. What they see, in any case, will be every bit as rare and not one bit less worthy of wonder. ❧ *(1995)*

North: The Boreal Wilds

Gray Ghosts

IN JUNE 1938, Henry Stelfox saw his first woodland caribou near the headwaters of western Alberta's Clearwater River.

"I approached to within sixty yards of them," he wrote later. "They were not afraid, they stood facing me, as if to inquire, "Well, what do you want?" Two of these caribou were magnificent specimens."

Caribou no longer live in the high country where Stelfox saw them. The Alberta government built an all-season road in the 1950s to make it easier for resource companies to exploit the timber, gas and other resources of Alberta's foothills region. The caribou soon succumbed to over hunting and habitat loss.

Stelfox, a volunteer Alberta Game Warden during the early twentieth century, reported that caribou also ranged the Bighorn Mountains north of the Blackstone River, the headwaters of Brown and Chungo Creeks, and the Coalspur area.

Like the caribou of the upper Clearwater River watershed, all are gone.

Today only a few small bands survive, all north of the Athabasca River. Alberta's woodland caribou population has dropped from as many as eight thousand in 1966, to fewer than two thousand today. In fact, says Dianne Pachal of the Alberta Wilderness Association, woodland caribou may soon vanish from Alberta's boreal foothills.

Caribou are wilderness animals. In a continent that passed from wilderness to post-industrial civilization in barely a century, caribou have consistently come out the losers. Woodland caribou no longer occupy their former ranges in Maine, New Hampshire, Vermont, Michigan, Minnesota, New Brunswick, Nova Scotia, Prince Edward Island and southern Ontario.

"The range of the woodland caribou has decreased considerably since the 1800s," says biologist Frank Miller of the Canadian Wildlife Service, "probably due to the destruction of climax forests and over hunting." Parasites carried by white-tailed deer can be lethal to caribou too. Deer invade caribou range as logging companies convert mature forests to second-growth.

So severely did caribou numbers drop in Alberta in the 1970s that the Alberta Fish and Game Association — a hunters' and anglers' club — asked the provincial government to cancel caribou hunting seasons north and east of Jasper National Park.

In 1981, the government closed the season. The decline continued. The following year, the provincial government officially designated caribou a "threatened species" — the first such designation in Alberta.

Closing the hunting season did little to halt the decline of caribou numbers, because hunting was not the major problem. Just like everywhere else that caribou have vanished, habitat loss was — and still is — the biggest problem facing the grey ghosts of the north woods.

North and east of Jasper National Park, industrial activity has increased dramatically since the 1950s. A major railroad and highway transect caribou migration routes and wintering areas. Oil and gas exploration cutlines crisscross the landscape, like jackstraws scattered through the forested foothills. Logging roads and clearcuts are now spreading across the last forested wildlands.

Jan Edmonds has spent most of the past decade following radio-collared caribou through the area's muskegs and mountains sampling feeding sites. She has measured lichen growth rates, autopsied dead caribou, and interviewed hunters, trappers and others who share the forested wilds with the elusive creatures. Her studies paint a bleak picture.

Edmonds found that caribou need old, unbroken forest. Slow-growing lichens typically festoon the branches of the ancient spruce and pine; other lichens cover the forest floor. These lichens are vital to caribou survival. Loggers, however, cut old trees by choice; in so doing they eliminate the lichens.

When logging opens the forest canopy, the openings create habitat for moose, deer and other animals that feed on deciduous shrubs and young vegetation. Higher densities of moose and deer support higher densities of wolves. Caribou — being easy prey — fall into a sort of "predator pit." Predators like wolves — their numbers supported by other, less vulnerable, prey species — kill more caribou than are born to replace the losses.

Clearing old-growth forests has other impacts on caribou too. If the clearcuts are large enough, they can interrupt the annual movements of caribou, isolating them from important parts of their range. New roads associated with forestry and mineral exploration are irresistible to hunters, who can quickly deplete newly accessible areas. While hunters can no longer kill Alberta's caribou, some inevitably fall prey to eager novices who mistake them for elk or other species.

Jan and her co-workers found one caribou that snowmobilers had evidently run down and killed for entertainment. Off-road vehicles rarely penetrate pristine forest, but where cutlines and forest development open new access into caribou habitat, snowmobiles, motor quads and dirt bikes soon follow.

Jan co-authored a caribou recovery plan for the Alberta government. Based on several years study, it identified habitat loss as the biggest long-term threat to the caribou, while predators, poaching and road kills were the chief short-term problems. Alberta Fish and Wildlife released the draft plan for public comment in 1986.

The plan called for no-hunting zones along several key roads; public education to reduce road kills and accidental killings by hunters who confuse caribou with elk or moose; long-term protection of key habitat areas from logging and motor vehicles; and a three-year program to reduce the number of wolves in key caribou areas.

Wolf control was the stumbling block. Fish and Wildlife's proposed wolf kill undermined the recovery plan's credibility with the public.

"I guess I was a bit naïve," Jan confesses now, reflecting on the uproar that resulted from her proposal for a three-year reduction in wolf numbers. "But if you look at the data, there was no other conclusion you could make. Predators are taking up to 19 percent of the adults each year. Calf recruitment is only 15 percent. If we are going to buy time for those caribou, there has to be wolf control."

Some environmentalists were willing to consider a one-time wolf kill if it would help the recovery of a threatened, non-game species. Nevertheless, the public outcry was sufficient to give Alberta politicians cold feet; the recovery plan remains "under study."

In 1986 Jan and her colleagues in the Alberta Fish and Wildlife Division's Edson office released a follow-up report identifying five critically important caribou wintering areas east of Jasper National Park. The report called for the Alberta government to protect two of these vital areas from any industrial activity. For the remaining three areas, it recommended special logging guidelines that would ensure a continuous supply of old forest and reduce access by motor vehicles.

That report, too, remains under study by the provincial government.

One thing that did not require so much study, however, was the Alberta government's decision to turn all five caribou winter ranges over to logging companies. In 1988 and 1989, Alberta launched a veritable blitz of new forestry projects across northern Alberta. Within one year, the government handed over a quarter of the province to the forest industry. The cut-rate for-

120

est giveaway was to supply wood to seven new or expanded pulp mills and some smaller lumber and particle-board plants.

Public uproar over wolf control paled in comparison to how Albertans reacted to the big forestry projects. A subsequent environmental review of one of these projects — the Alberta-Pacific bleached kraft pulp mill north of Edmonton — showed that the government lacked even the most basic inventories of fish and wildlife populations. The review showed that the government had no baseline data on forest ecology and had not consulted adequately with the public. In fact, most of the area so suddenly dedicated to wood fibre production was virtually unknown to government planners.

Where caribou were concerned, Jan Edmonds admits that nobody knows what shape most of the province's northern caribou herds are in. "We've only really studied the populations in the Hinton and Grande Cache area," she says.

"Woodland caribou," trumpeted a 1989 article in a widely distributed Alberta Wilderness Association tabloid, "may be extinct in Alberta within the lifetime of our children. They will be the first big game mammal extirpated in Canada in this century."

Jan Edmonds tries to remain optimistic. Nonetheless, she says, "All five primary winter ranges are scheduled for logging within the next twenty to thirty years." While the political debate over the future of Alberta's forests continues, Edmonds has turned to working with the forest companies who received cutting rights to the areas. She continues her research and correspondence with other caribou biologists across the continent, in hopes of finding ways to reduce the impact of huge forestry operations on an animal that needs old forest.

"Five years ago," she confesses, "I had a lot of confidence that we could do this, that we could manage for the long term survival of caribou. Now, I just don't know."

The special management guidelines recommended by Edmonds and her colleagues for three of the caribou winter ranges call for long forest rotations. Loggers would have to wait eighty to 150 years between clearcuts and limit the width of cutblocks to 150 metres or less. They would also leave unlogged buffers along streams and muskegs. The recommendations are based on an experimental logging strategy that Grande Cache Forest Products pioneered in the late 1970s.

Rocky Notnes, a Hinton-based outfitter and director of the Alberta Wilderness Association, feels the proposed guidelines should not apply to such a large area. "These are just experimental guidelines," he says. "What if they don't work, and they ruin the habitat? We will never get those caribou back."

Rick Bonar is a biologist who works for Weldwood of Canada, a pulp company whose kraft mill at Hinton controls an immense cutting area that includes primary caribou winter range. He disagrees with Jan Edmonds too, but he argues for bigger clearcuts, not forest protection.

"Fragmenting the habitat and keeping a third of it uncut may not be the best option," he says. "There are differences of opinions among biologists. It may be better to cut whole areas — big, progressive clearcuts — and then allow them to recover over a long period. That way you can ensure that there are always big, unbroken blocks of mature forest available to caribou."

Edmonds concedes he may be right. "Our recommendations may even be the worst case possible," she says, pointing out that understanding of woodland caribou ecology is still in its infancy. "We could save the lichen-producing habitat but mess up the predator-prey system."

Bonar feels that small cutblocks may create too patchy an environment. He points out that natural fires burn large areas in Alberta's foothills. Caribou have always had to adjust to changing forest cover patterns on a large scale.

Biologists agree, however, that logging is likely to have different effects on caribou forage than natural fire. Lichens take several decades to grow back after a fire. Fires usually leave patches of living trees and spars scattered across the landscape, providing a supply of lichen to recolonize the rest of the area. Clearcut logging, on the other hand, leaves a barren landscape and scarified (ploughed) soil — a much more drastic form of disturbance. Researchers only recently started looking into how well lichens regenerate after logging. By the time their results come in, the landscape of northern Alberta will have been changed forever.

The logging companies are not going to wait for answers. Rick Bonar argues pragmatically for designing clearcuts at least to look like burned areas. "If you cut on a whole-landscape basis, it actually looks more natural," he says, "apart from the roads."

The roads, however, are one of the thorniest dimensions of the caribou conservation issue. Traditionally, government resource agencies saw logging roads as a public benefit of forest development. New roads meant new access to fishing and hunting. Forest companies were loath to close roads, and government, in fact, demanded that they leave the roads open. However, once the trees were cleared, road hunters usually quickly depleted the newly accessible areas of wildlife. Remote road networks are also irresistible to poachers — a far more serious threat.

Alberta's pulp and lumber companies are aware of the growing level of public concern about caribou and other wildlife. Since the late 1970s one company — Grande Cache Forest Products — has experimented with an extended rotation system. Their approach ensures forest more than eighty years old always covers at least a third of their timber lease. Weldwood of Canada, which operates a pulp mill in Hinton, hired its first wildlife biologist in 1985. Weldwood is developing a logging strategy that takes into account the habitat needs of a variety of wildlife species including wilderness-dependent caribou and grizzly. If their plan works, it will be the first sign of hope for species like caribou whose ecology is totally incompatible with traditional timber management.

Conservationists remain skeptical, however. They point out that a corporation's first responsibility is to its shareholders. Deferring clearcuts on caribou range may be good for public relations, but it does nothing for the bottom line. The Alberta Forest Service still forces timber companies to liquidate old-growth natural forests and replace them with single-aged young plantations that have little wildlife value.

Perhaps the greatest cause for concern, however, is continued government failure to protect any habitat for wilderness-dependent wildlife. As early as 1979 government biologists identified key wildlife areas east of Jasper National Park. With the caribou recovery plan, and subsequent habitat plan, they refined these recommendations and gave them greater urgency.

To date, however, not one acre has been set aside for the protection of Alberta's first threatened animal. Loggers are clear cutting the Redrock caribou winter range. The A la Peche winter range has been partially logged under the Grande Cache Forest Products experimental system. Weldwood plans to log the South Berland winter range within the next decade.

The Prairie Creek winter range, recommended for long-term protection by the Alberta Fish and Wildlife Division, has been "under study" for two years.

The Alberta Forest Service handed over the Little Smoky River winter range — recommended for long-term protection by Fish and Wildlife and all major Alberta conservation groups — to Alberta Newsprint and Canfor Industries in 1988. The Forest Service belatedly agreed to consider a 30-year deferral of industrial activity in the Little Smoky, but Alberta Newsprint refused. Ironically, all used newsprint in Alberta ends up in landfills, since neither Alberta Newsprint nor any other companies have recycling mills. Newsprint made from caribou habitat is cheaper than newsprint made from newsprint.

Oil and gas companies continue to explore all five winter ranges in hopes of a big find which would lead, inevitably, to more roads and fragmented caribou habitat. During the exploration phase, however, government guidelines oblige the companies to rely on helicopter-assisted, hand cut seismic lines, and to refrain from activity during the caribou calving season.

Jan Edmonds continues to struggle with the increasingly-daunting task of protecting caribou in a landscape given over to the forest industry. Meanwhile, conservation groups futilely lobby government and industry to put the long-term security of caribou on at least an equal footing with the capital gains and dividend income of logging company shareholders.

History, however, has not been kind to Canada's woodland caribou. A future of massive forestry developments in Alberta's boreal wilds stacks stiff odds against the beleaguered animals. Rocky Notnes says, "If there were a real commitment to protecting the caribou, we'd have seen at least one major boreal wilderness area established. We would have at least that much insurance against the possibility of all these experiments failing. But there's nothing."

Henry Stelfox promoted the idea of a protected wildlife area in the upper Clearwater. His idea did not catch on with the government of the day. The caribou are gone.

John Stelfox followed his father's footsteps, devoting his life to conservation. Recently retired from a career as an ungulate biologist with the Canadian Wildlife Service, John was a member of a panel appointed by Alberta's Minister of Forestry, Lands and Wildlife. The Minister instructed the panel to review forest management concerns in the wake of public uproar over the recent Alberta forestry announcements.

The panel called for a large boreal wilderness area, echoing recommendations of public advisory panels, government biologists and conservationists over the past decade and a half. The government again dodged the issue. The official line is that wilderness-dependent wildlife can survive in a "multiple-use" landscape managed primarily for wood fibre production.

Across northern Alberta small bands of woodland caribou — unaware of distant arguments over their fate — continue to browse lichens and travel the quiet trails that stitch together their northern forest mosaic. From time to time they pause to sniff the strange odour of distant pulp mills. That smell is here to stay. The caribou, however, may not be. ❧ *(1991)*

Divvying the Berland

THE DAY IS ALMOST WARM for mid-January, the temperature hovering near freezing, but everyone knows a blizzard is coming. Here in the Rocky Mountains community of Jasper, few people take weather forecasts seriously. When the wind brings the stink of hydrogen sulfide, however, everyone knows that an Arctic storm is bellying up the Athabasca valley from the Berland country.

Sixty miles north of Jasper, the Athabasca River escapes the last of the Rocky Mountain Front Ranges to begin the second leg of its 2,000-mile journey to the Arctic Ocean. In doing so, it leaves Jasper National Park and ceases to be a Heritage River. Once in provincial lands, the Alberta government puts its rivers to work. They are available for whatever industrial purposes the Alberta Department of Environment will permit. The department takes a pragmatic view of rivers: it calls them water resources.

At Hinton, ten miles downstream from the national park boundary, a pulp mill belches out a double load of pollution. The bitter wind that drives the first snow pellets up-valley toward the mountain wall catches plumes of sulphurous steam from the mill's twin stacks. Below, tea-coloured effluent pours into the Athabasca, discolouring it and filling the air with a sewage odour.

The Champion Forest Products [now Weldwood of Canada] kraft pulp mill is the largest single point source of pollution on the Athabasca River. So much waste flushes into the river that cancer-causing chemicals contaminate river life for hundreds of kilometres downstream. The government's premise for licensing so much pollution is that several downstream tributaries swell the already large Athabasca and help dilute Champion's lignin compounds, chlorine, dioxins and other pollutants.

Ninety-six kilometres downstream, the Berland enters the Athabasca from the north. A Canoe Alberta reach report says: "On arrival at the Berland River confluence, the contrast between the clear Berland and the polluted Athabasca is evident. Along the whole tour, the river water is not considered drinkable ...." Upstream from the confluence, however, the Berland is sweet and clear.

The Berland and its tributaries — the Wildhay River, Pinto and Hightower Creeks — drain a vast area of rolling, forested foothills and muskeg plateaus north of the Athabasca River. Their gravelled runs and quiet meanders support populations of native rainbow trout, some of Canada's most southerly Arctic grayling, and huge bull trout.

Few who fish the Berland and its tributaries care to hike in from the road. In the Hinton area, off-road motor vehicles are generally considered more prestigious than walking boots. If you work at the Champion Forest Products mill or on a cutting crew, chances are that you can afford to buy an all-terrain cycle or

127

quad. Oil and gas exploration cutlines and new logging roads penetrate the muskegs and sidehills north of the Athabasca. There is always somebody who can give you a tip on how to get in a little farther than you thought you could.

Nonetheless, the country is still pretty remote. Grizzlies roam the floodplains. Deer, moose and elk are common along the aspen sidehills and alluvial meadows. In winter small bands of woodland caribou — like the grayling, a northern species occurring only this far south in Alberta's foothills — forage in the old spruce and pine forests for lichens.

Perhaps the most unique animal population in the area is a herd of mountain goats. More than seventy miles from the nearest mountain, a small band frequents the forest edges along Pinto and Hightower Creeks. If the country were less remote, the goats would probably have vanished long ago, easy victims of poachers.

The Champion pulp mill is only an occasional irritation, when the wind is from the south, to the goats bedded on the cutbanks overlooking Pinto Creek, or the caribou quietly foraging in the snow-muffled forest along the Berland. Life goes on pretty much as it always has in the Berland country.

For now. Change, as well as hydrogen sulphide, is in the wind.

It is summer now: July, 1987.

I stop at a service station fronting on Highway 16 in Hinton. A woman runs my credit card through her machine and hands me the slip to sign. The pulp mill smell is on everything.

"Sure can smell Champion today," I say.

She sniffs and shrugs. "We call that the smell of jobs."

The line is not original, but I smile. It is true, after all. Champion employs several hundred people at its mill and in the bush. Hinton is typical of many Canadian towns. Its counterparts can be found from Tumbler Ridge to Kenora, and from

128

Port Alberni to Baie Verte: resource industry towns dependent on the cyclical demand for their commodities, and sullenly protective of the companies that sustain them. In Hinton, the commodities are coal and timber.

The town council tries to promote tourism, too. It hasn't caught on — tourists don't seem to like the smell of jobs.

Outside, the sun has disappeared into haze. The Rockies lie silhouetted against a yellow sky. Traffic is heavy on the Yellowhead. Truck drivers, impatient with the 60-km speed limit through town, use their engine retarder brakes to take revenge on the residents. Motel, restaurant, service station and equipment dealer signs glare along the highway strip. A pickup truck cuts me off and its young male occupant gives me the finger. I don't know why.

I'm in town to spend the evening at the Legion Hall. Champion Forest Products has organized a public meeting to release a draft environmental impact assessment on its planned mill expansion. The company wants to double its mill capacity to take advantage of the growing demand for bleached Kraft pulp. Paper companies use bleached Kraft pulp to produce high-quality paper for printing books like this one.

More than fifty people in the Legion meeting room sit facing a table full of Champion representatives. The meeting is orderly and polite. Bill Gunning, the company's acting technical superintendent, explains the pulping process in great detail and describes the new pollution controls Champion will install.

The crowd, however, is restive. They ask a few questions about pollution almost as if they feel obliged to do so, but this is obviously not what they came for. Some seem irritated when they learn that the company's statistics — which imply pollution levels will drop once the new mill's modern technology is up and running — disguise the truth. The expanded mill will produce more pollution. Despite some exasperated muttering, interest in

129

the mill is clearly slack. These folks are used to the smell of jobs.

Only when the floor is opened to questions does it become apparent what is on people's minds. To feed the expanded mill, Champion has to cut more wood. The company is negotiating an expanded harvest area, and has surveyed two roads into the area they have in mind.

They already control three thousand square miles. They want twelve hundred more.

The map on the display panels shows the existing harvest area and the newly surveyed routes. One cuts through caribou winter range. The other bypasses the Pinto Creek goat herd. Both extend well north of the Berland.

The president of the Alberta Fish and Game Association has made the long trip out from Edmonton. A hunter in the crowd asks if Champion is willing to keep a gate on the new roads. He insists that only aggressive access control will protect caribou, goats and other game from over hunting, poaching and legal harvest by Treaty Indians. The company representatives say that the government will not allow them to gate the roads.

A representative of the Alberta Wilderness Association stands up and formally requests that the company enlarge the EIA to include the forestry operations, rather than just the mill expansion. He gets no encouragement. Another member argues for total protection of caribou winter range from the chainsaws. He gets even less encouragement and merely succeeds in setting off a company forester on a long sermon about how cutting old forests guards against pine beetles. The old forests are spruce.

Sitting quietly beside the wilderness advocates and fish and game contingent, several men look out of place in so formal a setting. One, a hawkish-looking individual with long black hair and a heavy wool jacket, stands and introduces himself as a fur trapper. He looks like he wishes he were somewhere else; most of us feel that way by now.

130

"The problem is," he says, "you're after mature timber, and we need mature timber. We try to manage our harvest just like you do: on a sustained yield basis. The seed areas we leave are the old timber where the older martens live and breed. The animals we trap in the younger stuff are the surplus, the ones that get pushed out of the old forest. But you're telling us that you cut the old stuff first."

This time, the Champion representatives bend a little. They agree to meet separately, later, with members of the Alberta Trappers Association to discuss how to avoid conflict. However, one points out, "We have two fundamental principles we operate by. One is that you balance the haul distance from year to year. The other is that you cut the old growth first."

The meeting runs out of steam quickly. Outside it is nearly dark. Everyone wants to go home. An air of palpable cynicism has settled among the ranks of the wilderness contingent. They have been here before.

It has become apparent, in the course of the evening, that Champion is interested in efficient, industrial timber production. They are willing to discuss any wildlife species that can adapt to early-successional vegetation. Anyone concerned about old-growth forest, caribou, fur-bearers or other values unlikely to survive in a landscape dedicated to wood fibre production must talk to the government departments that regulate the forest industry.

Driving home, it occurs to me that most of those present at the meeting had at least one piece of common ground no matter how divergent their views.

All discussed the Berland in terms of its resources. The argument was over who would get how much of the pie. Nobody talked about what kind of pie they were divvying up, but everyone wanted a fair share.

To the north of my little ribbon of a highway, in the dark beyond the hills, the Berland is chattering quietly to itself, just as

131

it has always done. In its cold backwaters, schools of grayling are picking mayfly nymphs from the limestone cobbles. Perhaps wolves are howling at the edge of a floodplain meadow. If so, the elk and deer will be listening, stilled for a moment by the reminder that their deaths wait somewhere beyond the shadows.

Live hard, you guys. You're resources. Your time is going to come.

February 1988. Champion has already cut the new roads. The government has approved the pulp mill expansion. Now a Japanese firm has announced plans for a huge new pulp mill at Peace River, to the north. Everyone is excited. It all means more investment, more jobs; more timber commitments.

The pie has been divided. As usual, the largest piece went to those who created the most new jobs — especially smelly ones. Next year the new roads will bring rifles deeper into caribou winter range. Soon the trees will start to fall.

"There wasn't even a road to Grande Cache twenty years ago," the Metis trapper told me after last summer's public meeting. "Now those damn quads and dirt bikes are everywhere in there."

I guess he'll need one of those new jobs, soon.

Another winter storm is on its way; I can smell Hinton this morning from my Jasper back yard.

The smell takes me back to the first time I floated the Wildhay, one of the Berland's chief tributaries, by canoe. It was nine years ago. There were no trikes then. There were still a lot of native rainbows and grayling to be caught. I remember sitting up one evening to watch the water ripple quietly by in the shadows beyond the fire. A coyote shrilled in a meadow down the river. The smell of Hinton's pulp mill was in my nostrils again that night, as it no doubt was in his.

That was the smell of jobs. I didn't want to believe, at the time, that it might be the smell of the future. But we all belong to a culture where we grew up believing that wealth and abundance are honourable rewards for those who exploit the fruits of the frontier. New roads are a way of life in Alberta. Progress is a religion. Progress means new jobs.

There are still some wild and beautiful places in the Berland country. There are trout that have never fled from an angler, and caribou that have never dodged a bullet. There is still a bit of the wilderness frontier left.

Live hard, you guys. We're creating jobs, and jobs vote. You don't. And while fifty people attended the public meeting where we argued over how to divvy you up, nobody even thought of asking where we got the right to do it. ❦ *(1988)*

A Place of Ghosts: The Prairie

Whoopers

I AVOIDED MR. VANDERWAAL as much as I could that fall. It wasn't easy, since he helped at our place a lot after Dad caught pneumonia. But if facing Dad was hard for me, talking to Mr. VanderWaal was almost impossible.

When I shot Mr. VanderWaal's cow, he didn't act all that upset. It was Dad who wouldn't let go of it. He took away my gun. "You get it back when you can convince me you deserve it," he said. "A gun is not a toy. You don't make mistakes with a gun."

I still don't know how I hit that stupid cow. I was shooting gophers along the edge of the coulee, down past the correction line. They would stand up at the edges of their burrows squeaking at me. At the shot they collapsed, kicking, in the dust or dropped down the hole.

I had twelve gopher tails and was just heading back for the road when I spotted two gophers. They were chasing each other about at the edge of the big field Dad had just finished seeding to winter wheat. Both ducked into a pile of rocks. One came out and stood up.

I sat, settled the sight on the base of his little rodent head, and squeezed. He dropped, twitching, and at the same moment there came a horrible bawling from the coulee. I stood up. Sweet Jesus, one of Mr. Vanderwaal's cows was thrashing about in the buckbrush a quarter mile down the coulee!

Her calf ran to her and nudged at her side. She tried to stand and collapsed again. I felt sick to my stomach. My bullet had put her down; I hadn't checked behind my target. I also knew that nobody shoots a cow by mistake.

I thought of running away from home, pretending to be sick so nobody would find out who shot her, even — for a moment — of shooting myself. In the end, though, I could find no way out of facing Dad. I jogged for home along the fence line.

We drove over and picked up Mr. VanderWaal. Dad was too mad even to talk to me. Mr. VanderWaal gave me one long look and then ignored me. I sat between them and felt like a piece of crud.

The cow had stopped struggling when we got to her. Her belly was wet with dark blood and covered with flies. I hung back as the men leaned over her.

"She's a goner," Mr. VanderWaal said.

"Shit." Dad flashed a look at me.

Mr. VanderWaal took his rifle from the truck. He fed one brass shell into the chamber, and closed it. He held the end of the barrel a couple inches from the back of her head. The cow's eyes rolled, bulging with mindless cow-fear as she tried to watch all of us at once. The calf pleaded hungrily from the coulee-bottom. The rest of the herd watched solemnly.

At the blast, the cow went rigid. One eye bulged half out of her skull and stayed there, horror fading to blankness. Her whole body stretched. One hind leg flexed, kicking. The leg reached, stretched, tense as if it were trying to resist what had already happened, then dropped limply. Blood dripped from her shattered mouth.

I threw up. Neither of them even looked at me. I had never seen something die like that before; not the dozens of gophers I had murdered for a dime a tail, nor the chickens whose heads Mom so matter-of-factly hacked off, nor the partridges and prairie chickens Dad and Mr. VanderWaal shot each fall down along the coulee.

Later, after we had hauled the quartered carcass back to Mr. VanderWaal's place, Dad gave me his lecture about guns.

By then I had begun to feel persecuted. I had only

138

made a mistake, after all. It hadn't been like the guys from town. They came out every now and then and shot up signs and mailboxes and things deliberately. It wasn't as if Dad had never made mistakes.

Like the time he and Mr. VanderWaal shot the whooping cranes. He had been a lot older than I when they did it. He had known it was against the law, too.

We had a picture of the dead cranes in one of the family albums. Dad was holding one at arms' length by the neck. Its feet scraped the ground. Mr. VanderWaal was grinning. Dad had a mustache and his face was rounder and smoother than now. I could not help thinking he looked like somebody I wouldn't like if I met him today.

I studied that picture a lot after they told me about shooting the cranes. It was like a cipher. If I examined it long enough maybe, I would find some clues about what Dad had been like when he was younger — who he had been.

We had been hunting prairie chickens the day they told me about the whooping cranes. It was an Indian summer day, the coulee slopes red and gold with the fall colours of saskatoon, chokecherry and buckbrush. We already had seven or eight chickens when we stopped for lunch.

They were talking about how they used to hunt ducks in the stooks, before the days of the big combines. "They used to just pile in," Mr. VanderWaal said. "All you had to do was throw out a couple dozen tarpaper decoys, burrow down in the stooks and wait."

"Remember the whoopers we shot that one time?"

They had been sitting huddled into a stook in light drizzle. It was after sunset and the light was nearly gone. The only way to see the ducks was to look for dark shapes moving fast against the clouds as they arrived, wings whistling in the wet, gabbling quietly to one another as they set their wings and dropped toward the tarpaper outlines below.

Dad shot and saw a duck fold. It fell with a thud among the stooks a dozen yards away. He was standing to retrieve it when Mr. VanderWaal grabbed his arm and pulled him back.

"What?"

"Look."

Ponderous and heavy, wings lifting and falling in great slow-motion beats, seven huge birds materialized from the rain mist. They were flying so low that they had to lift, one by one, to cross the fence line.

One croaked, and then the others began to call, a resonant, two-noted trumpeting.

They flew in staggered single-file, each riding the turbulent wash of another's wingtips. They were so white they could have been mirages, ghosts out of the Pleistocene past. Their wings hissed and creaked, up, down, up, down, as they passed within a dozen yards of the watching hunters.

At the last, without a word being spoken — probably without a thought being thought — Dad and Mr. VanderWaal stood up. The cranes were so close, Dad said, that even in the poor light he could see their heads turn, the primitive little eyes suddenly aware of the men.

Both men shot. Three birds fell. Two were dead when they hit the ground but one jumped to its feet and ran with long, awkward steps into the dusk, dragging one huge, snowy wing.

There were only two cranes in the photo. "You never found it?"

Mr. VanderWaal shook his head. "Coyotes must of got it or something. I never even saw a feather when I went back the next day."

"Never seen a whooper crane since then, either," said

Dad. "They were even pretty rare then. Most of them were further east."

"Geez they were pretty things," said Mr. VanderWaal.

It was something about the prehistoric look of those two huge birds, something in the way they seemed to represent a time already past when grain was stooked rather than swathed, when ducks darkened the fall skies, when Dad had a mustache and went hunting on horseback with his school buddies. I kept going back to study that picture. Dad had an old leather wallet full of brightly coloured wet flies his own dad had left him; they gave me the same feeling. There was something important back there that I had missed.

I don't know what I wanted. Lots of those little sandhill cranes were still around. Sometimes I would stop and watch them, turning them into whooping cranes, putting unbroken prairie and undrained sloughs into the big grain fields. But they were not much bigger than geese and I usually saw them on the winter wheat the same as the big honkers that came up off the river each fall. It just didn't work.

I would look at Dad, his lined face, whiskers like steel filings on his cheeks, the bald spot on his head, and try to picture him young and unmarried. It was impossible. He was my dad; he had always been. I don't even know why it mattered. For some reason I just really wanted to know how it had felt to be young at a time when there were whooping cranes to shoot.

We had no shortage of sandhill cranes around, the fall he caught pneumonia. It was a wet one. The grain was sprouting in the swaths and it was mid September before a chinook blew the fields dry enough to combine. Meanwhile, the ducks, geese and cranes got fat and happy on the swathed grain and the sprouting winter wheat.

Mr. VanderWaal lost time on his own land because of the time he spent on ours. Dad lay in the hospital in town and

141

watched the sky outside the window, or paced the halls cough-
ing. He was not used to being sick. The germs seemed to take
advantage of his inexperience. After the first week and a half he
rarely got out of bed at all, but just lay there and tried to sleep.

I didn't like visiting him at the hospital, although Mom
insisted. I still felt rotten about the cow. So did he, especially
since he had to sit there feeling useless while the man whose
cow I had shot did his work for him. That's how I figured he
felt, anyway. He hardly ever mentioned the work he couldn't
do. Mostly he either slept, coughed, or talked about the early
days when he had been starting on the farm.

I wish I hadn't shot that goddamn cow. I would have
spent more time with him.

The rain had ended. The skies were clear, everything
fresh-washed and golden in the late afternoon sun when I
looked out the school bus window and saw the big white birds
way out in the winter wheat. I could see three, and one smaller
reddish one. Sweet Jesus: whooping cranes!

The bus turned the corner at the correction line. They
were gone from sight. "Damn!" I said.

Mom was on the phone when I busted into the house.
She didn't look up, just motioned for me to be quiet. I found
Dad's binoculars, dumped my books on the couch, and headed
back out. Mom put her pale hand over the phone receiver.

"Don't go taking off," she said. "I need you here."

"I'm just going up the coulee a little way." The door
had slammed before I had finished the sentence.

Thinking about it now I'm almost embarrassed with
how worked up I got over those things. It was like I was not
even myself, I was so charged with adrenaline or whatever it was
that swelled my face and sent my feet flying effortlessly across
the ground. The excitement was almost sexual. For four birds. I
can't remember having ever felt like that before, or since.

142

A big pasture of unbroken prairie stretched down from the bluff behind our house to the coulee. It was easier running than the field that stretched from the house to the big field, and shorter than going around by road. I flew across the close-cropped prairie grasses, dropping to roll under fences and skipping over badger and gopher holes. Rose prickles and thistle leaves filled my socks. I barely noticed them.

A quarter mile down the coulee I figured I must be just about even with the birds. I slowed to a walk and began to climb the slope, heart pounding in my head. I could barely breathe, more from suspense than exertion.

Over the rim. Nothing there. The field was empty.

Sweet Jesus: too late.

I felt sick with the letdown. I did not even know for sure that they had been whooping cranes. Maybe they had just been swans or waveys.

Then I heard a resonant trumpeting unlike anything I had ever heard before. It was like someone blowing over a bottle top, but higher, louder and more rolling, a sound that made the sky vast and the distance empty. I shaded my eyes with my hand, staring desperately…and there they were.

They were in flight, already half a mile off, flying straight away. All I could see was the white flash of wings as they caught the sunlight on each up-stroke. With each down-stroke they disappeared into sky glare.

I watched them going, sick with regret. I willed them to come back, and I knew that they wouldn't. It was out of my hands. They were gone. White over gold, flicker, vanish, flicker, vanish; until at the last moment they veered to bypass our buildings and disappear for good behind the poplar windbreak. Even then, their great rolling cries drifted back to me out of the empty sky.

If I had stayed at home, they would have gone right over me.

I stood still. Nothing stirred. The whole prairie was gold and black, utterly still. The sky was barren. The whoopers no longer called.

My stomach felt sick. It was like when Mr. VanderWaal had finished off the cow and I had watched it trying not to die when it was already too late and nobody could change what had happened.

How could I have missed so narrowly something I wanted so badly? How could they have gone just then, when I was so near — when it was that important to me?

You can't call things back. You can't turn time back. You can't ever have the things you missed. And when I saw our pickup pull out into the road and accelerate down to the correction line, then turn and disappear behind the swell of land that hid town from view, I ran again, back down the coulee side and through the wet grass toward the house. Only now my feet no longer flew. What I ran toward was gone. ❧ *(1988)*

Save the Gopher!

AS A YOUNG BIRDWATCHER, I used to ride my bicycle out into the prairie from my home in Calgary. It was a world of wheat, grainfields and scattered sloughs. Black terns and avocets shrieked overhead as I hunted for their nests or waded through the cattails looking for bitterns and sora rails.

My bird books told me that some prairie birds were rare. Those were the ones I was most eager to find. Most of those birds needed natural habitats, however, and little native prairie survived near Calgary even then. The birds I found were weedy species that could live on the leavings of prairie agriculture or around the wetlands that still survived.

One day, as I explored the sandstone outcrops along Beddington Creek, I heard a hawk screaming near a small grove of poplars. At my approach it flapped away from a large stick nest and wheeled overhead. It was a large pale hawk with a reddish-brown V where its legs crossed its abdomen.

My field guide told me it was a rare ferruginous hawk — a species now on Canada's threatened species list. I returned often to watch from a distance where I would not disturb the hawk and its mate. They hunted the heavily grazed native prairie along the creek bottom, bringing back one gopher after another to feed their hungry little babies.

Watching them, I wondered why this overgrazed valley was the only place for miles around where ferruginous hawks nested. I didn't know then that the abundance of gophers in the native grassland pastures lining Beddington Creek accounted for those hawks' success that year. Ground squirrels make up more than 80 percent of the ferruginous hawk's diet in Alberta.

It is not easy to discuss any endangered prairie wildlife without talking about gophers — okay, Richardson's ground squirrels, if you want to be fussy about names. Real gophers are the creatures some people call moles and few have ever seen. Real gophers live virtually their entire lives underground.

Most prairie Canadians prefer to call Richardson's ground squirrels gophers. They are stubby little rodents that run around the edges of fields or stand erect at the mouths of their burrows. At a distance, gophers look like tent pegs or picket pins.

Try to picket your horse to one of these pins, however, and it will squeak and vanish into a hidden maze of underground runways. Generations of gophers have learned that there is little profit in standing still for a human being.

Humans, for the most part, do not like gophers. The first gopher squinting into the March sunlight each year, of course, is in a different category from your ordinary gopher. That first one is a sign of spring. The problem is that they keep on coming after that until it seems like prairie sprouts gophers faster than it does wheat or barley. By early May, it can seem like gophers are just about everywhere.

Gophers eat wheat and barley. They are rodents, after all. They also eat garden vegetables and other green things. They dig burrows and throw the dirt up into conspicuous mounds, often in the middle of golf course runways or newly planted lawns. Gophers breed prolifically: up to a dozen babies each year, year after year. All those babies dig holes and eat crops too.

It doesn't take much exposure to gophers before the average prairie-dwelling human develops a serious interest in finding ways to cut down the population.

There are many ways to kill gophers. If Richardson's ground squirrel was not such a prolific breeder and so proficient at colonizing new terrain, it's a safe bet the species would be on Canada's endangered species list along with the ferruginous hawks that eat them. In fact, we humans have already wiped out ground squirrels from some parts of the prairies.

Flooded out of their burrows and snared with binder twine, gassed in their dens, shot with .22 rifles and killed with poison-laced grain dropped down their holes, ground squirrels face endless persecution at the hand of man.

Life was already rough for Richardson's ground squirrel before modern agriculture turned it from a native rodent to a pest. Many animals like to dine on the plump and abundant little creatures.

Badgers snuffle about at night, sniffing out the fresh

scent of sleeping ground squirrels, then digging them out. Coyotes sometimes tag along and wait nearby in case the badger's quarry tries to make a dash for it out the back door. Even without the unwilling assistance of a badger, coyotes catch many ground squirrels. Long-tailed weasels specialize in hunting ground squirrels, as did the now-extirpated black-footed ferret.

Bull snakes hunt ground squirrels and kill them by squeezing them in their coils, like boa constrictors. Overhead, hawks circle patiently, watching for unwary survivors. Ground squirrels are larger than the more numerous mice and voles — a heartier snack — and they are active during the day. Most other prairie animals come out at night, when hawks cannot find them.

Bald eagles appear to time their spring migration to coincide with the emergence of the first ground squirrels from their winter dens. What could be better, after a long flight north, than to snack on small, furry hors-d'oeuvres? The little animated snacks must be easy to find as they stand squinting into the spring sunshine, silhouetted against melting snowdrifts.

No wonder ground squirrels spend so much time standing upright, squeaking nervously. They live under perpetual siege.

Geoff Holroyd is an endangered species biologist with the Canadian Wildlife Service. He says that few people realize the importance of the humble gopher. "Not only are ground squirrels a critical link in the web of life that sustains endangered and threatened species such as the ferruginous hawk," he says, "but ground squirrels play a vital role in keeping many other predators off the endangered list."

Biologists Laurie Hunt and Robyn Usher conducted a satellite-imagery study of an area along Alberta's lower Red

147

Deer River to learn more about the relationships between ground squirrels and predators. They found that ground squirrel colonies occupied less than 3 percent of the landscape, mostly native prairie that had not been ploughed up for cropland. Ground squirrels from that tiny portion of the whole landscape provided up to 94 percent of the food supply for prairie falcons that nest in the area. The ongoing war against ground squirrels, combined with continuing conversion of native prairie to cultivated cropland, may help account for the fact that barely half as many prairie falcons survive in Alberta as did thirty-five years ago.

The prairie falcon, one of the most spectacular wild hunters of the plains, is a dusty-brown raptor nearly the same size as the better-known, and endangered, peregrine. Prairie falcons nest on ledges on the cliffs that line prairie rivers and coulees, and range widely in search of their favourite prey: Richardson's ground squirrel.

Holroyd notes that federal and provincial governments have spent hundreds of thousands of dollars to bring back the peregrine falcon, with mixed results. Meanwhile, conservation agencies virtually ignore the prairie falcon, though acting now to protect a mere 3 percent of the prairie landscape could go a long way to ensuring its continued survival.

"It's far easier," he says, "to keep species from becoming endangered in the first place than it is to bring back a species once it's already become endangered."

Will we only begin to worry about the prairie falcon after the last pockets of ground squirrel habitat are gone?

That is what happened with the burrowing owl, a species that may be on the fast track to extinction in Alberta. Like the ferruginous hawk, the burrowing owl is another endangered species I first met during childhood bicycle excursions beyond the outskirts of Calgary.

One afternoon, while I was idly counting ground squirrels on an overgrazed pasture, I spotted two strange-looking creatures standing on a ground squirrel mound. My binoculars revealed two long-legged little owls, staring at me through fierce yellow eyes. One bobbed up and down, then flew a short distance to land on a fence post. The other vanished suddenly into the ground!

Two pairs of burrowing owls nested in that heavily grazed native pasture. Scarcely bigger than ground squirrels themselves, burrowing owls nest underground in abandoned ground squirrel burrows. They eat grasshoppers and insects that thrive in the same shortgrass habitats that ground squirrels prefer.

Since ground squirrels prefer low-growing vegetation, they benefit from grazing. No doubt before Europeans arrived in prairie Canada, ground squirrels relied on plains bison to keep the grass down. Burrowing owls line their nests with bits of dry cow dung — evidence that bison, ground squirrels and the animals that depend on ground squirrels probably evolved as a single community of life.

Burrowing owls need ground squirrels, but that is not all they need. The burrowing owl may be doomed in Alberta for other reasons: the extensive use of toxic pesticides for grasshopper control and the continuing proliferation of roads and highways. Cars and trucks kill the little owls when they flutter across the path of passing vehicles. Irrigation expansion in southern Alberta continues to eliminate the native prairie essential to this unique little owl. Burrowing owl numbers, as a result, have declined by up to 70 percent in less than a decade.

Unlike the burrowing owl, the swift fox may be on its way back from extirpation. Their hopeful future is the result of reintroduction programs supported by the Canadian Wildlife Service, the Calgary Zoo, and provincial wildlife agencies. Like the burrowing owl, swift foxes benefit from abundant ground squirrel. Swift foxes hunt mostly at night, so ground squirrels do

149

not form an important part of their diet. Ground squirrel burrows, however, give the little predators a place to live. Swift foxes take over the burrows and enlarge their own use.

Mice, bull snakes, rattlers and weasels all make their homes in ground squirrel dens too.

Many prairie Canadians think of gophers as vermin. Ecologists, however, have begun to describe Richardson's ground squirrel as a keystone species in what survives of the Great Plains ecosystem.

Cleve Wershler, a well-known prairie ecologist, goes as far as to describe the much-maligned ground squirrel as the "wildebeest of the prairies" — a dramatic comparison at first glance, but close to the truth.

Wildebeest, on the East African plains, feed lions, hyenas, vultures and a host of other species. Their grazing maintains the natural mix of vegetation. They fertilize the land with their dung and shape it with their hooves. Without the wildebeest, the great pageant of life many of us picture when we imagine eastern Africa would not be possible. The wildebeest ties that ecosystem together. Remove it, and the whole thing falls apart.

We have already lost an important force in the prairie ecosystem, the bison, and with it the prairie wolves and grizzly bears that relied upon the bison herds.

In much of what remains of the prairie West, ground squirrels play every bit as important a role as wildebeest still do in the Serengeti, and bison once did here. Take away the lowly gopher and a whole suite of other species that depend upon it for vital elements of their ecology would follow the ghosts of the wolf and grizzly down the empty halls of nostalgia and regret.

Yet, for the past century, we have worked hard to eradicate ground squirrels.

What if we had succeeded? ❧ *(1996)*

THE FIRST PHEASANT FLUSHED as the kitchen door slammed. Dad and his cousin, whose farm we were visiting, scrambled to slide shells into their double-barrels as Gordon and I raised a chorus of excited shouts.

"There's one, Dad!" I yelled, assuming that since he was more than ten he must be blind.

"There's two more!"

"Holy! Look at them all!"

Dad gestured furiously for his loudmouthed kids to pipe down. Too late: at least fifty pheasants exploded from the side of the coulee below the house. Albert just shook his head.

A few independent-minded birds were still in there, however. By the time the dog had worked to the head of the coulee Dad was well on his way to another limit of five cock pheasants.

That was 1962, and Alberta's Western Irrigation District was a paradise of pheasants and Hungarian partridges. The landscape was a patchwork of flood-irrigated hay fields, leaky ditches lined with big poplars, tangles of buckbrush and rose, and sloughs full of cattail and sedge. It was almost perfect pheasant habitat, and an idyllic place for Dad and his young sons to hunt through the long autumn seasons into late November when the snow began to drift.

Driving home in the evening, Dad sometimes talked about his youth. He described clouds of ducks darkening the sky and sharp-tailed grouse sailing above the shrubby sandhills north of Strathmore. I would watch the shimmering lines of northern mallards strung out like shifting signatures on the sky and feel deeply, fervently, a part of this vast and beautiful landscape and the prairie heritage to which my father was introducing me.

Even then, however, wildlife habitat was under siege.

Today, with more than 90 percent of the original prairie already gone, even the weedy habitat diversity introduced by early irrigation farming is vanishing. Many hunters have written off Alberta's irrigation country as a lost cause.

Last fall my friends Glenn Webber and Jim McLennan hunted hard all day in the same country I tramped as a child. After finding not a single pheasant with their pointers, they stopped at a Buck for Wildlife habitat project near Namaka. They took some pen-raised chukars out of the trunk, and gave their pointers some practice on the tame birds.

"This," Glenn said when he told me later, "is not how it's meant to be."

There may yet be hope for Alberta's over-exploited croplands. Ironically, the very forces that have destroyed so much wildlife habitat are now being put to work to restore some of what has been lost.

The Canadian Pacific Railway started a few showcase irrigation projects to help attract more prairie settlers in the late 1800s. Since then, irrigation canals have spread across southern Alberta to the point where the area now has two thirds of Canada's irrigated farmland. Irrigated farms cover almost 500,000 hectares of southern Alberta. When the CPR was unable to make a profit from irrigation, the government took over. It has been subsidizing the industry ever since. During the 1950s, the Prairie Farm Rehabilitation Administration built several large dams and canal systems. In the 1970s, Alberta's Environment department took over irrigation development.

In the last decade alone, government water engineers have quietly poured more than a billion dollars of public money into irrigation infrastructure.

Irrigation is a godsend to farmers who must contend with periodic drought on Canada's western plains. Dams and weirs divert water from prairie and foothills rivers, especially

152

during spring floods, into large canals. Elaborate water supply systems store the diverted water in reservoirs, then feed it out through canal systems to the farmers' fields during the hot, dry summer. Some canals put return flows into rivers at their downstream ends. Others drain into the open prairie, spilling leftover water into natural lowlands.

Irrigation subsidies have created a bottomless thirst for cheap water in southern Alberta. Every large river now has at least one major dam to trap and hold the spring runoff.

The PFRA dammed the St. Mary's River southwest of Lethbridge in 1952. The St. Mary's Irrigation District has since become one of the most productive agricultural regions in Alberta, covering more than 132,000 hectares of what was once native prairie. However, the St. Mary's River now flows as a mere trickle each summer. Its cottonwoods are dying. The valley's wildlife wealth is depleted. The river's fishery is devastated.

Off the river, farmers drained and filled wetlands and converted coulees to water storage reservoirs — again, with government money. Alberta Fish and Wildlife Division biologists studied one small portion of the St. Mary's Irrigation District in the mid 1970s. They found that more than two thirds of native upland habitat vanished into cropland between 1964 and 1974. Subsequent studies show that southern Alberta's irrigation country has lost as much as 75 percent of what wildlife habitat remained in the mid 1970s.

The St. Mary's Irrigation District has become a biological disaster area.

In its earliest stages, irrigation development actually benefited wildlife. Until the 1970s, farmers relied on gravity to deliver water from ditches to fields, which meant that they frequently left upland areas uncultivated. The original irrigation ditches were leaky. Hybrid poplars, willows, rose, buckbrush and other native and introduced vegetation colonized the ditch banks and seepage areas on the downhill sides of ditches. With the vegetation came growing numbers of white-tailed deer, pheasants, partridges and a host of other wildlife species that formerly had only survived along creek bottoms and river valleys.

In the 1970s, however, new irrigation technologies arrived on the scene. For the first time, farmers could irrigate land uphill from the canals by pumping water into huge sprinkler systems. Demand for water increased in leaps and bounds. Both government agencies and local Irrigation Districts began to look for ways to send more water to crops and less to wildlife and weeds.

Since 1976, Alberta Environment has pumped more than a billion dollars into irrigation projects that replace wildlife habitat with more crops. Water engineers lined canals with plastic or cement to reduce seepage. Meanwhile, they bulldozed down poplar stands and closed hundreds of kilometres of secondary ditches. In southern Alberta they dammed the Oldman River and began planning for more dams on Willow Creek and the Little Bow River.

Every improvement in irrigation system efficiency translated directly into new wildlife habitat losses.

The big new centre-pivot irrigation systems require big fields. Buying the expensive pipes and pumps forced many farmers into debt. Their need for cash flow drove them to intensify their farming and eliminate any unproductive corners that were not helping to pay off their loans. Farmers created space by tearing out fence lines and filling small wetlands: more habitat loss.

Thousands of hunters visit irrigation country each fall. They could not help noticing the changes.

Pheasant populations crashed in the late 1960s and continued to decline through the next decade. Duck numbers plummeted through the 1970s and 1980s. The Alberta government, responding to hunters' concerns about habitat loss, tacked a surcharge onto hunting and fishing licenses and created a new Bucks for Wildlife Fund. The government earmarked the money for habitat restoration projects.

Still, for Alberta's understaffed Fish and Wildlife Division, new funding was not enough to solve the problems of habitat loss. They also needed land and water, or the cooperation of others who controlled land and water. Instead, irrigation upgrading projects financed by Alberta Environment and Alberta Agriculture continued to destroy habitat faster than Fish and Wildlife could restore it.

"We dealt with those agencies for two years to try to get them to plan for the needs of wildlife too," says one provincial biologist. "We simply asked that they consult with us at the planning phase and use our technical advice. We made overtures at every level right up to the Ministers. Nobody wanted to hear about wildlife."

Finally, Fish and Wildlife staff approached the managers of several Irrigation Districts. It seemed unlikely that they would get a sympathetic hearing. Irrigation Districts are privately managed and controlled by irrigation farmers with a personal stake in water supply projects.

However, both the Eastern Irrigation District (EID) and the Bow River Irrigation District (BRID), northwest of Medicine Hat, proved ready and willing to cooperate. Today, some of Alberta's finest Bucks for Wildlife habitat projects are in these two irrigation districts. In several cases, in fact, new habitat resulted from canal improvement programs that would otherwise have resulted in big losses.

Fish and Wildlife staff are now involved in irrigation planning before Alberta Environment's water engineers. It is a refreshing change.

Steinbeck Slough is a prime example of what can happen with irrigators are willing to add biological expertise into the old "sun, water and the hand of man" irrigation equation. The slough — the flooded bottom of a long coulee adjoining the East Branch Canal in the EID — once frustrated irrigators and biologists alike. Each spring, when Alberta Environment engineers diverted water into the canal system from the Bow River, the canal overflowed into Steinbeck Slough. Until the slough filled, there was too little pressure to force water through the rest of the canal system to downstream storage reservoirs, rendering the whole system inefficient.

In summer the slough dried up, leaving it nearly useless for waterfowl and other wildlife since any vegetation that sprouted in the spring inevitably died back in the summer drought.

When the Eastern Irrigation District upgraded its East Branch Canal, one of the highest priorities was to block the overflow into Steinbeck Slough. However, based on advice from Alberta Fish and Wildlife biologists, the engineers chose not simply to block the mouth of the coulee. Instead, they installed a simple water control structure that fills Steinbeck Slough each spring and keeps it wet through the summer. Today the slough is a productive wetland, and the canal is more efficient.

Working with irrigation districts can pay habitat dividends, but private landowners hold the key to protecting existing habitat. One Fish and Wildlife study found that 42,000 acres of high quality habitat remain in southern irrigation districts. About 80 percent of that is in private ownership. Only cooperative ventures with private landowners can offer lasting hope for these.

South of Brooks, I saw one wetland that was due to disappear before Fish and Wildlife developed such a cooperative joint venture agreement with the owner. A small feeder ditch led to a dugout that supplies domestic water for a farm family across the road. The Bow River Irrigation District wanted to replace the whole thing with an underground pipe, to improve efficiency. However, since Fish and Wildlife's Habitat Development Branch had the opportunity to review the project in advance, they proposed an alternative deal. Fish and Wildlife kicked in $10,000 from the Bucks for Wildlife Fund and the farmer agreed to upgrade the dugout, then fence it and the surrounding prairie for wildlife habitat.

Where private landowners do not wish to cooperate, or cannot afford to, wildlife interests have to be able to buy land. Habitat acquisition is expensive, however. Funds are scarce even though more than a third of Alberta's Bucks for Wildlife funds go to the Southern Region.

"Bucks for Wildlife is stretched as far as it can go," says Lorne Fitch, Regional Biologist for the Alberta Fish and Wildlife Division. He and his staff have mapped out tracts of critical habitat and high priority opportunities for habitat restoration, but they lack both funds and political support to follow through. Provincial and municipal politicians have no interest in proposals to develop a Conservation Strategy for the region. No provincial laws exist to protect biodiversity or habitat for endangered species. Lacking clear policy support, Fish and Wildlife staff can only pick away at the edges of a very big problem. As each year's Bucks for Wildlife funds come available, Habitat Division staff focus on securing or rebuilding the most vital habitat areas and wildlife dispersal corridors.

Fitch sees Bucks for Wildlife as venture capital for habitat. He takes pride in the fact that for every Bucks for Wildlife dollar his staff spends, they attract two to three dollars in outside funding. Fish and Wildlife technicians have developed a fine instinct for spotting emerging opportunities to make deals for wildlife.

"One thing is for sure," says Fitch, "if anyone were to come up with more money, we have the projects ready to go now."

In one recent case, the Canadian Wildlife Service found itself with a small cash surplus at year's end. Lorne Fitch and Harry Vriend had already identified a piece of high-quality prairie scrubland with a marsh sustained by irrigation return flows. Within days, they had secured the Bobby Hale Marsh — three quarter sections of critical wildlife habitat.

All across southern Alberta, small patches of high-quality habitat are beginning to reappear. Most are the result of cooperation among landowners, some irrigation districts, and the Alberta Fish and Wildlife Division. With the recent launch of the massive North American Waterfowl Management Plan, new money has now begun to flow in. Wildlife biologists are optimistic that the long-overdue task of reversing the ecological destruction wrought by intensive irrigation development in southern Alberta may already have started in earnest.

I asked Lorne Fitch if he felt there was any real hope for restoring the lost habitat and wildlife diversity of Alberta's irrigated farmscapes. After a little hesitation, he said that he believed there is.

"The time is ripe for these sorts of projects, and the foundation is already in place," he said, referring to the growing sense of cooperation among Irrigation Districts, private landowners and government, and public demands for environmental restoration. "One of the problems we face in trying to build a higher profile for these sorts of projects is the public perception that southern Alberta is a desert anyway. People figure there was never much here to lose. The truth is, this is one of the most biologically productive areas in the province, and the one where a small effort can yield the greatest payoff.

Especially when there is irrigation water available."

Fitch agrees that no habitat development projects can replace the rich, self-sustaining wildlife ecosystems destroyed by on-stream dams like the St. Mary's and Oldman. Nonetheless, he is optimistic about the prospects for turning around the more recent loss of wetlands and pheasant habitat.

If he is right, it can't come a moment too soon for one who remembers the glory days of the 1960s. ✣ *(1994)*

Quality

THE OLD FARMSTEAD IS ONE of the last remaining patches of pheasant cover in a countryside that teemed with ringnecks not too many years ago.

I never knew the people whose failed hopes the weathered old buildings represent. They had moved away well before my time. Large piles of stones, buried now in spreading caragana bushes, suggest that they did not fail for want of industry. A lot of labour went into making their fields safe for cultivator blades.

Whatever their story, they are gone. Only decaying buildings remain amid a wilderness of caragana run wild.

It is the caragana that makes the old place important to the few wild pheasants that remain in the area. When winter snows carpet the surrounding fields and Arctic winds sweep down across the plains, few shrubby corners remain where pheasants can find shelter. The farmstead's abandoned caragana windbreaks are among the only winter refuges that survive.

Caragana is a tough shrub, native to the Old World. It arrived in prairie Canada during the late 1800s. Caragana is so

159

well adapted to drought that it thrives long after those who planted it move on. So hardy is this introduced legume, and so good at sheltering pheasants, that conservationists often use it in habitat projects. They plant caragana to restore some habitat diversity to the monotonous farmscapes we have allowed too much of the prairie West to become.

Farmland without pheasants is a dreary place compared with farmland with pheasants. What could be more laudable than to plant a few caraganas?

Reflection suggests, however, that caragana is merely a first step, and a short step, on the road to restoration.

Less than a mile from the old farmstead, I know of another place that still holds a few pheasants. This one is a natural slump: a steep broken hillside covered with chokecherry, saskatoon, rose, hawthorn and buckbrush. Like the old farmstead, its shrubby tangles stand against the winter winds, offering shelter for the poorly adapted Chinese ringnecks during the toughest time of the year.

Unlike the old farmstead, this tangle of shrubs consists of native species that belong with the landscape: Canadian prairie plants. Elsewhere, such vegetation has given way to wheat, barley and canola. Here it survives in a place too steep and poor to cultivate.

From a pheasant's point of view, I suspect, the brushy old hillside and the brushy old farmstead are about equal. Both serve just as well when the north wind blows. From a pheasant hunter's point of view, perhaps the old farmstead comes out a bit ahead. It is on flat ground and hunting between the planted rows of caragana is easier.

Nonetheless, this pheasant hunter finds himself drawn more strongly to the rough terrain and impenetrable tangles of the old slump. When a hunting partner asked me why, I concluded that it was a question of quality.

160

Recently, trying to find a way to define that quality in my own mind, I drew up two lists. One was a list of the plants, birds and mammals that I know to use the old farmstead. The other is a list of those that use the hillside.

Regarding woody things, the hillside is ahead five to one. It does even better in other categories.

The old farmstead has a heavy cover of brome grass and dense patches of Canada thistle, Russian thistle, goosefoot and sweet clover. All, like the caragana, are introduced plants. In summer, it offers shelter to the endangered loggerhead shrike, perhaps because the shrikes hunt the introduced house sparrows that nest in the old granaries. Robins, goldfinches and vesper sparrows nest in the farmstead too.

The hillside, on the other hand, has a mosaic of plant communities containing, in total, more than a hundred species of native plants and many introduced plants that agriculture has added to our prairie flora. Twenty-six species of birds, at a minimum, nest on the hillside. One reason for this diversity is that native birds are adapted to native habitats. Another reason is that habitat diversity offers more ways of making a living. Mule deer live year round on the hillside; they only appear occasionally in the old farmyard. There is, as best as I can figure, at least twenty times as much biological diversity on the natural hillside than down at the abandoned farm.

Come hunting season, the wind has an empty sound as it hisses through the monotony of brome grass around the old farmstead. Sometimes a magpie or a sullen grey owl goes rattling out of the leafless caraganas. For the most part the old place is forlornly still.

Up on the hillside, however, waxwings and late robins feed on dried saskatoons and chokecherries. Migrating tree sparrows and whitecrowns lisp shyly in the undergrowth. Chickadees forage in the hawthorn branches. Rough-legged hawks hang overhead, searching for meadow voles and deer mice. While the dog wears herself out trying to decode the trails of pheasants in the tangled shrubbery, I find myself at home again amid the ecological riches that are prairie Canada's natural heritage.

On balancing the books, then, it seems to me that the attraction of that hillside pheasant cover is obvious. The old farmstead is a richer place than the surrounding grainfields, but the natural hillside is several degrees richer yet.

The family that farmed that old place does not farm there anymore. They were swept away long ago by the tidal wave of twentieth-century change. They left behind a pile of rocks, several rows of caragana gone wild, some pheasants, and far too little of the natural wealth that was there when they arrived.

Today, some of us work to rebuild pheasant populations by restoring shrubby habitat. The return on our efforts, I suspect, will relate to how we define that work. If the work is merely to plant pheasant cover, then caragana will do. However, if we define our work as the restoration of natural wealth to wounded landscapes, then pheasant recovery becomes only one of many dividends. This latter is likely to prove a complicated, fascinating, and far more rewarding enterprise.

Ducks Unlimited used to employ water engineers to restore ducks. Their reasoning was that ducks needed water. It helped some ducks. Eventually, DU changed its program focus to nesting cover, working with tame hay, alfalfa and other exotics. That helped some ducks, too.

In the 1990s, DU now plants native grasses and restores small, natural wetlands. They have adopted more of an ecosystem, rather than a duck-factory, focus. The ducks will benefit at least as much, if not more, from this latest approach. So, too, however, will godwits, longspurs, pipits, buntings and the many other native species left out of the earlier duck habitat projects.

There is a subtle difference between habitat development and ecosystem restoration. Both produce ducks, or pheasants, or whatever the targeted game species might be. Only one, however, restores landscape quality, natural diversity, and the richness that was, and can again be, prairie Canada. ✧ *(1994)*

Down by the River

Clogged Arteries

AS ONE SLIPS QUIETLY DOWN the last slack
reaches of the Parsnip, the roar of the Finlay
Rapids, a couple miles down the Peace, breaks
upon the ear in a slow crescendo.... Ahead, and
beyond the big shingle bar, fast water is playing
strange tricks in the dancing mirage; it is of a
new colour and it is moving from left to right,
shearing off, as with a knife, the sluggish current
of the Parsnip. And that is where the Peace is
born....

R. M. Patterson, *Finlay's River*, 1968

The birthplace of the mighty Peace River now lies beneath the still waters of British Columbia's largest artificial reservoir, Williston Lake.

The same year that R.M. Patterson's book about the wilderness rivers of B.C.'s Rocky Mountain Trench was published, the floodgates closed on the 182-metre W.B. Bennett Dam, plugging one of Canada's greatest rivers. The dam drowned more than sixteen hundred square kilometres of forest, rapids and fertile bottomland forever.

Almost half a century before Patterson first ventured up the Peace to its headwaters, Vivian Pharis' grandparents floated down the Parsnip into the Peace River. A few miles downstream they found their new home on the fertile river floodplain twenty miles above the Peace Canyon.

Vivian Pharis spent much of her childhood on their wilderness ranch. "It was the most beautiful ranch I have ever seen in the world," she says. "My grandmother had an acre of garden where she grew field corn, cucumbers, tomatoes — things we can't even grow here in Calgary. The hay grew four feet high — over my head when I was a little girl."

By the 1930s, the Goldbar Ranch had its own post office and school, and a population of thirty. "Many were the trappers who spent their summers at the ranch," says a local history book compiled in 1973. "They preferred the farm with its freedom, its jollity and its bounteous home cooked meals, to life in town."

In 1968 the ranch, too, disappeared under the flood.

"I think that was what turned me into an environmentalist," says Pharis. At the time she was a university undergraduate. Today she is president of the Alberta Wilderness Association, one of the province's oldest and best-respected conservation groups. In the years since floodwaters erased her family's home, the A.W.A. has fought and lost a series of battles to stop dams on other Alberta rivers. It failed to save the historic Kootenay Plains from a hydropower dam on the North Saskatchewan River in the early 1970s. A few years later, it tried and failed to stop the Dickson Dam from plugging the Red Deer. Nothing daunted, the A.W.A. continues to fight an irrigation dam under construction on the Oldman River in southern Alberta. The association's efforts, thus far, have saved Alberta's Milk River from the dam builders.

The great forests of the Peace, Parsnip and Finlay Rivers were only partially cleared before the Williston reservoir filled. "Some of those cottonwoods along the river were more than eight feet in diameter," says Pharis, "but they only took some of the best timber from the slopes."

Deadheads — sodden timber that has drifted loose from the flooded valley floor — remain major hazards to boat travel on the reservoir today, and on other reservoirs dating from the same period.

"Twenty years ago," admits Dr. Anthony Tawil, an engineer with Acres International, an engineering firm that represents Canada on the International Committee on Large Dams, "we didn't clear reservoirs. Now, that was an incredibly stupid way to operate, and we don't do that anymore. Now we clear them as a matter of course."

Flooded timber, farmland, homes and scenery, however, are only a few of the social and ecological costs of plugging living rivers with cement and fill. Some costs turn up miles away, years after the controversy surrounding each dam's construction has faded into history.

Several hundred miles downstream from the Bennett Dam, the Peace River meets the Athabasca River. There, in the far northeast corner of Alberta, the two rivers form one of the largest freshwater delta in the world where they empty into Lake Athabasca. Each year, swollen by runoff from melting snow and seasonal rains, the two mighty rivers flood over their banks, spilling across the delta. River silt enriches delta soils and floodwater replenishes shallow basins and marshes, raising the water table.

Too much flooding can turn the perched basins into open lakes and drown fertile shoreline areas. Too little, and they dry up. Under normal conditions the annual flooding cycle produces up to 19,000 kilometres of rich, well-vegetated shoreline throughout the delta. As many as 600,000 young ducks and geese fly south each year from the delta's mosaic ecosystem. Millions of muskrats remain behind. Almost two thousand Cree and Metis people sustain themselves year-round on the delta's walleye, goldeye and pike populations, trapping thousands of muskrats each winter.

While the Williston Reservoir was filling behind the Bennett Dam, the massive spring floods that have sustained the delta for millennia suddenly dried up. Without the floods, perched bogs and ponds dried up. Productive wetland communities shrank, replaced by dry grassland and sedge. Open sedge meadows, in turn, dried up and gave way to dense willow thickets and spruce.

The prolonged drought devastated fish and wildlife populations.

Faced with a continuing environmental disaster, the B.C. government reluctantly joined the Alberta and federal governments to find a solution. The solution, predictably, employed more dam engineers and involved more damming: the governments built two weirs on major delta channels. The weirs artificially duplicate the effect of the Peace River's former spring floods in backing up floodwaters from the undammed Athabasca.

Although the artificial weirs only restore floodwaters to part of the delta, the Peace-Athabasca Implementation Committee reported in 1987 that the weirs had successfully restored a near-normal flooding cycle. Vegetation, muskrats, fish and waterfowl appear to be responding to the restored rhythms of the delta. Wood bison that winter in the delta's vast sedge meadows are benefiting too.

Yet this may be only a temporary solution. Another hydroelectric dam — temporarily deferred for economic reasons — waits in the wings. The Alberta government wants to build a dam on the Slave River rapids, below the delta. As the river backpools behind the dam, it will inundate critical bison ranges. The downstream effects of the proposed Slave River dam may impoverish the entire Mackenzie River valley.

Most people, to the extent that they even think of dams as hard on rivers, assume that the damage is confined to the area flooded by the reservoir. However, as the case of the Peace-Athabasca Delta shows, one large dam can radically alter a whole river. In his classic textbook *The Ecology of Running Waters*, Dr. H.B. Hynes says: "The influence of a large dam is…profound and it extends a long way downstream."

Government and industry build dams for many reasons. Hydropower, irrigation, water supply, flood control and lake level stabilization are among the most important. In every case, engineers promote dams as a means of controlling water resources. The problems hinge on the fact that a river is not a water resource: it is a living ecosystem driven by running water. Change the flow of water, and we change the whole system.

Hynes describes rivers as dynamic, complex ecosystems. River water changes as it flows down its channel, picking up dissolved minerals, sediments and heat. The flowing water erodes or deposits silt, sand and gravel in predictable patterns, depending on how fast the water flows and how much sediment it carries. Because water flows at different speeds in different parts of a channel, a natural river bed is a mosaic of habitats sustaining many species of algae, invertebrates and fishes.

Spring floods bring fresh deposits of sediment to replace those washed downstream. The floods enrich the floodplain with silt and moisture, sustaining plant communities and a host of wildlife. The floodplain's trees and other vegetation, in turn, produce shade and food for stream life.

Running water is merely the common thread that binds the river ecosystem together. A river's ecological complexity is almost beyond comprehension. Hydraulic engineers can begin to predict a dam's impact on the water and its bed — although even here reality often surprises them — but they usually fail to predict the intense ecological damage dams inflict on downstream ecosystems.

In a 1987 study Dr. Stewart Rood, an ecologist at the University of Lethbridge, examined aerial photographs and measured forest stands along three small rivers in southern Alberta. He found that dams can ultimately destroy the most productive ecosystems in prairie Canada.

Rood found that the Belly River — with only three small weirs that do not affect spring flooding — still has cottonwood forests as lush and abundant as they were a quarter of a century ago. The Waterton River, however, has 25 percent fewer cottonwoods than it did before water engineers dammed it, in 1964, to supply water for irrigation farmers. Just a short distance away, the

St. Mary's River has fared even worse. Dammed in 1951 for irrigation water supply, the St. Mary's has lost more than half its original cottonwood forest. Its valley is turning into a dry coulee.

The loss of riparian cottonwood forests is a serious matter on the dry plains of prairie Canada. The huge trees provide shade and shelter for deer and breeding habitat for orioles, raccoons, owls, herons, and countless other species of wildlife. More than three quarters of all prairie wildlife species depend on riparian habitats for part, or all, of their lives. Cottonwood leaves, shed by the billions each fall, provide organic debris that keeps rivers fertile and productive.

World Wildlife Fund Canada's Prairie Conservation Action Plan describes prairie riparian ecosystems as "some of the most threatened ecosystems in arid and semi-arid regions of the world." It predicts that, without remedial action, cottonwood habitats may disappear by the end of the next century.

Rood suspects the big trees are dying because government water engineers draw too much water out of the rivers every summer to meet the needs of irrigation farmers. Some prairie rivers run nearly dry in mid July downstream of irrigation dams. Cheryl Bradley's research on the Milk River, however, suggests that the problem is more complex.

One of the most magnificent prairie wildernesses remaining in North America is along the Milk River canyon in southern Alberta. The river's headwaters are mostly in Montana. It swings north into Alberta near Lethbridge, then flows another 200 kilometres along the southern edge of the province. South of Medicine Hat, the river swings back into Montana. There it encounters the Fresno Dam.

Cheryl Bradley conducted painstaking studies of cottonwood groves both upstream of the Fresno Dam, in Alberta, and downstream, in the USA. She found that cottonwoods sprout on the insides of meander bends where silt accumulates, year after year, while the river erodes the outsides of bends.

Spring floods make meander bends migrate, year after year, across the floodplain. In the process, old cottonwood stands fall victim to the hungry waters eroding the outside of each bend. The same waters, building the opposite point bars up, leave bands of maturing cottonwoods behind as point bars grow. Cottonwoods, over millennia, have adapted their life cycle to line up with the behaviour of the river; they release their seeds in late spring when prairie rivers are in full flood. Their timing ensures that new generations of cottonwood trees will sprout on rich, wet, newly deposited silt that the floodwaters have spread across the point bars.

The whole floodplain is a living, dynamic system.

Below the Fresno Dam, Bradley found that cottonwood groves were aging. New seedlings were scarce. As old trees died, they were not being replaced. The forests were in trouble.

A river's ability to carry silt in suspension depends on its ability to keep moving. When water piles up behind a dam, its silt load settles out. The water coming out of the dam is clean and hungry; the river promptly sets to work restoring its silt load. It does this by eroding the river bed.

Downstream from the Fresno Dam, the Milk River's meanders no longer migrate. Instead, the river is slowly cutting downwards, entrenching itself in the channel it was following when the engineers who built the Fresno Dam closed its flood-gates. Old cottonwoods are now high and dry as the water table follows the river downward. The new point bars that cottonwood seedlings rely upon have become rare and unreliable, choked with weeds and often dry just at the most critical season.

The dam, of course, has benefited farmers who use the stored water to irrigate barley, alfalfa and other field crops in an area notorious for its unreliable summer rains. But the river, deprived of its silt, its seasonal cycles, and much of its water, is no longer able to sustain its once-rich ecosystem.

To Nelbert Little Moustache, a Peigan native from the Brocket Reserve on the Oldman River, the loss of floodplain cottonwoods is more than an ecological disaster. It is a cultural and religious sacrilege. The cottonwood tree is a central element of the religion and traditions of the Blackfeet people. Already declining among every dammed river in western North America, some of the healthiest and most extensive stands of plains cottonwoods still thrive along Alberta's Oldman River. The potential loss of their sacred forest is one of many reasons why the Peigan continue, with Pharis' Alberta Wilderness Association, to wage an underdog battle against the Three Rivers Dam, currently nearing completion on the Oldman.

If the Oldman's cottonwoods die, the last healthy stands in Canada will be on the Milk River. And Alberta's water bureaucrats have already drafted plans to dam the Canadian reach of the Milk River. The plans are waiting on the shelf for the right political moment.

The downstream ecological effects of dams aren't widely understood and, until recently, have not been important factors in motivating communities to rise against dam-building. Most of the opposition to dams in Canada has centred on either the value of the areas those dams will flood, or the damage those dams will cause to fisheries. Plugging a river wreaks havoc on most fish populations.

On the positive side, some dams have created valuable cold-water fisheries on rivers where they didn't exist before. In the American southwest, rivers like the Green and Columbia were once too muddy, volatile and warm for trout. Today, with predictable flows of cold water released from the cold bottom layers of reservoirs, these rivers are the sites of productive recreational fisheries. Their native fish species, however, are mostly either extinct or endangered because of the impact of dams and cold water on their habitats.

On balance, history has shown that large dams cause far more damage than good to river fisheries. Canada's Department of Fisheries and Oceans, in 1986, released an assessment of the likely impacts of ALCAN's proposed Kemano Completion project in British Columbia. The scientists reported that in 75 percent of the eighty-one cases they studied, flow changes had hurt natural trout and salmon populations. They identified several different ways in which dams hurt fishes.

The most obvious impact — the one that killed the once awe-inspiring salmon runs of the Columbia River basin — is that dams physically block migrating fish. Salmon, bull trout and other species heading upstream to spawn in cold headwaters are doomed to frustration if they encounter a dam. Even in cases where engineers installed fish ladders or electric companies trap spawners and truck them around the dam, few spawners get through. Young salmon, returning downstream, die when hydroelectric turbines grind them into fish food, or when nitrogen gas churned into the water in turbulent dam tailraces poisons them.

Dams change downstream water temperatures because, unlike natural lakes, most release cold, oxygen-poor water from the bottoms of their reservoirs. Sudden releases of cold water — a daily occurrence below most hydro dams — can kill food organisms, fish eggs and fish because of drastic shifts in water temperature and pressure. Dams cause upstream habitats to clog up with sediment that settles out of the ponded water. Blocked by the dams, fine gravels no longer enrich downstream reaches; fishes there gradually lose their spawning beds. Some dams also pollute downstream river water because organic waste or heavy metals accumulate in the reservoirs.

The ecological costs of damming a river are staggering. So why do we build them?

More than half of Canada's large dams were built to gen-

175

erate power. Energy utility companies often call hydroelectricity — since it does not rely on burning fuels — "clean" energy. The great dams of the Columbia River project and the more modern dams of Robert Bourassa's James Bay Project fall into this category. Ask the rivers, however. They know that no energy comes without an environmental cost. Hydropower is far from clean.

The Columbia River project, for example, destroyed one of the greatest salmon spawning runs in the world. Almost 80 percent of the 748 kilometres of river that once flowed in Canada have vanished beneath reservoirs. Arrow Lakes reservoir flooded some of British Columbia's only Class "A" agricultural land. Thousands of square kilometres of the most productive forest land in B.C. have been lost forever and — as on the Peace — the dam-builders left most of the trees standing, uncut.

Anthony Tawil agrees that Canadians have paid some high environmental prices for cheap hydropower. He argues, however, that there is little point in dwelling on the mistakes of the past. "Most publicity on dams is bad," he says. "Partly it's because in the past we have done some very destructive things. But partly it's because engineers have not done a good job of communicating. There have been some very beneficial results from dams."

Tawil cites flow regulation as a downstream benefit that improves the river environment. Spreading out a river's flow so that more water runs during the critical low-flow periods of mid-summer and late winter can give aquatic life with a more stable environment. It also produces recreational benefits throughout the year. Fluctuating flows caused by a network of hydropower dams on its headwaters nearly destroyed Alberta's Bow River. Since the 1950s the Bearspaw Dam, just upstream from Calgary, has regulated its flow. The Bow is now one of the most heavily used urban recreational rivers in Canada. Its rainbow trout fishery is world-famous. Flow regulation paid off for the Bow — but

176

only because other dams had devastated it.

The International Committee on Large Dams is compiling a report that will assess both the benefits and disadvantages of large dams, according to Anthony Tawil, "…to try to provide a more balanced view."

The Committee's report is not likely to sway Vivian Pharis. She points out that whatever benefits dams may deliver to consumers, on-stream dams almost inevitably hurt rivers and riparian ecosystems. She insists that water management should emphasize reducing water demand, and using existing supplies as efficiently and frugally as possible. While she recognizes the need to divert some water from rivers into off-stream storage reservoirs — which deliver many of the same benefits with far fewer ecological costs — she remains adamantly opposed to damming rivers.

"We have lost rivers, valleys and ecosystems that should have been protected as national treasures," she says. "Maybe we didn't know enough about the environmental costs of big dams, back in the 1950s and 60s. But today we do."

Cliff Wallis, president of the Friends of the Oldman River, points out that decades of experience have shown that large dams don't even deliver the economic benefits that their proponents often boast about. "In the United States," he says, "water agencies have found that by investing in technologies that use water efficiently, they can increase available water supplies just as much, at a tenth of the cost."

Tim Palmer — an American journalist whose book Endangered Rivers and the Conservation Movement examined the history of dam building and river protection in the U.S. — agrees. Most often, he says that the costs of building a dam vastly exceeded initial estimates, while proponents consistently overestimated economic benefits. Growth in demand for power and water has not matched projections. New technologies, growing costs and increased public commitment to conservation, according to Palmer, have turned the tide against large dams in the United States.

There is, simply, no need to waste money and rivers anymore.

Tom McMillan, Canada's former Minister of Environment, has called for more sensitivity to the values of rivers, and new approaches to meeting the water and power needs of society. In 1987 McMillan released a Federal Water Policy that states: "…Canadians have tended to undervalue instream uses in their water management decisions, with very expensive long-term consequences. Canada's rivers are a priceless and irreplaceable part of our natural and cultural heritage."

Nonetheless, a century of freewheeling development and economic growth has left many Canadians with a sort of benign indifference that works against river protection. If we continue to demand cheap, abundant water and power, we cannot expect to save our surviving rivers.

John Thompson, a Calgary-based resource economist, points out the logical inconsistency that often undermines our efforts to protect rivers from ourselves. It does not show much serious commitment, he says, to leave the sprinkler on in the yard and the light on in the hall while we go canoeing all weekend, only to come home Sunday night and write an angry letter to a politician about the mismanagement of a favourite river.

The value of Canada's surviving wild rivers and riparian ecosystems derives not only from their ecological complexity, historical significance and intrinsic worth but, sadly, also from their rarity. Most Canadian rivers are already dammed. Work continues today on dams on Alberta's Oldman, Saskatchewan's Souris, and Quebec's LaGrande. Government water developers may announce new dams soon for Alberta's Milk, North Saskatchewan and South Saskatchewan, Manitoba's Assiniboine and Nelson, and British Columbia's Stikine.

Peter Pearse, Chairman of the recent Inquiry Into Federal Water Policy, underscored the scarcity of free-flowing rivers in a 1984 speech to the Canadian Water Resources Association. He reminded the engineers gathered there that, "…the Fraser is the only major river in southern Canada that has escaped damming."

Vivian Pharis has no photographs to remind her of her family's wilderness ranch on the upper Peace River. She shows photographs of Williston Lake reservoir instead: a vast expanse of steel-gray water stippled with floating logs and surrounded by vast clearcuts. There is a deadness to the pictures. The water no longer dances.

I asked her if she feels bitter about her family's loss. She shook her head.

"I suppose we didn't know then what we do now about the waste and damage that a big dam represents," she said. "The important thing is to recognize that we no longer have that excuse. And there are very few free-flowing rivers left in Canada today."

Today, in the waning years of the 20th century, our understanding of river ecosystems has barely begun to catch up with our technical capability to exploit them. Understanding and humility, if they come, will be too late for the hundreds of river reaches lost to reservoirs or forever impoverished by the more subtle impacts of dams.

It is time to save the few that remain.   *(1991)*

The Tree and the Trout

Each fall, when cottonwood leaves turn yellow and begin to set sail on the October breezes, brown trout come up the Bow. Some turn and ascend the Elbow River to spawn below Glenmore

Dam. Others remain in the Bow, forging upstream through Calgary, Alberta to spawning beds in the backwaters and riffles below the Bearspaw Dam.

By the time the first ice begins to form around streamside boulders, another spawning season is over. The trout retreat to their wintering holes to wait out another long winter.

Seasons come and go along the river; the trout spawn and return; the years roll by.

Although I grew up only three blocks from the Bow, it was not until I was in high school that I first fished the big river. It was a challenge for a boy who had grown up fishing small headwater creeks. Nonetheless, I soon learned how to catch the abundant little rainbow trout in the long riffles upstream from the Crowchild Bridge.

I was an aspiring fly tier with a nervous dog. His tail developed a zigzag, patchy look during my Bow River phase. Each time he saw me coming with the scissors he would cringe and try to tuck his tattered tail beneath his belly. I tied flies that I called "bucktails," for lack of a better term. "Dogtail" was not in any of the books I had read. It was a simple pattern: little bits of Tim's tail tied onto a hook wrapped with Christmas tree tinsel. I anchored the whole thing down with Mom's sewing thread and my brother's model airplane glue. It worked just as well as the more expensive creations I could not afford and lacked the skill to tie.

Each evening after supper, I grabbed my fly rod and headed down to fish the river till dark. Throughout September, I usually managed to catch the odd little rainbow. By mid-October, however, when streamside foliage was golden and the river full of floating, soggy leaves, the rainbows no longer fed so eagerly in the evenings. Drifting leaves, like submerged booby traps, confounded my fishing as the streetlights flickered to life across the river. I sometimes fished several minutes before realizing I was casting a piece of sodden vegetation. Rafts of brown and yellow foliage eventually blanketed the eddy at the toe of my favourite run, making it virtually impossible to fish.

One evening I let my homemade fly drift into the accumulation of leaf litter. There was a bulging of the river's surface, so subtle in the near-dark and streetlight-flicker that I almost missed it. I set the hook instinctively, and was suddenly fast to a big trout.

The fish pulled me helplessly after him as he ran, sulked, ran and held again, working steadily downstream toward the dark outline of the Crowchild Bridge. At length I wrestled him ashore. I raced home to show the biggest fish I had caught until then — an eighteen-inch brown trout — to Mom and Dad.

When I think back on my finest brown trout fishing trips, the picture that comes to mind always seems to have poplars in it. Golden cottonwoods lining the Bow River late in the fall; balsam poplars turning silver in the wind as a June thunderstorm rolls across the Fallentimber; the glistening, summer-green foliage of black cottonwoods crowding the lower Crowsnest.

The biggest browns hide beneath logjams formed by old cottonwoods, washed out by spring floods. What do you snag your backcast in? Poplars. Where do the salmon flies and golden stones take refuge in the short weeks between the crazy fishing of the stonefly hatch and the equally crazy fishing of the egg-laying flight? The poplar canopy.

Anglers fish all day surrounded by wind-chatter in poplar foliage, then lean against the grooved bark of an old cottonwood for lunch. The vireos and orioles that serenade June mornings — background music for countless great fishing trips — nest in the cottonwood canopy. In the grassy, windblown outer foothills, eager anglers watch for ribbons of green showing where their favourite trout streams burrow through sheltering galleries of poplar forest — black cottonwood, Plains cottonwood, narrowleaf cottonwood, balsam poplar.

It is more than mere coincidence that cottonwoods and

brown trout live together in the landscape, and in our minds.

Cheryl Bradley studies forest ecology in southern Alberta. Several years ago she became curious about why cottonwoods were growing scarcer along many rivers both in Canada and the USA.

Cheryl mapped the native range of the plains cottonwood, the largest and most spectacular of the poplar family. All along the western edge of its range the cottonwood lines some of the most famous trout streams in North America: the Missouri, Big Hole, Beaverhead, Yellowstone, Platte, Bighorn and others.

Those are potent names in the minds of most serious trout anglers. As a teenager, I used to buy back-issues of the big three American sporting magazines at a used-book store in Hillhurst. After covetously poring over accounts of great Montana and Wyoming trout rivers, I would go down to the Bow and fish beneath the cottonwoods. I had no way of knowing at the time that the only difference between my rivers and theirs was that nobody had written mine up yet.

Like the famous American rivers, the Bow is full of big browns and rainbows. Like those other rivers, cottonwoods line its banks. And like most of those other rivers, Cheryl learned, the cottonwood stands are gradually dying out and failing to replenish themselves.

Recently, several anglers who regularly fish the lower Bow River began calling for action to protect the river's cottonwoods from beavers. At several points along the river below Calgary, the rodents continue to fell the big trees. There are few young poplars to replace them. Some anglers wrap chicken wire around the bases of trees near the water's edge to deter the beavers.

The problem, however, is not beavers. And, as Cheryl Bradley's graduate research revealed, there may be little we can do to save those beautiful floodplain forests.

The Milk River — where Cheryl did her earliest research — supports at least as many beavers, and far more cottonwoods, than the lower Bow. Most springs bring a new crop of cotton-woods to replace those lost to beavers or washed out by spring flooding. Along the Bow, however, springtime usually brings few washed out trees and fewer cottonwood seedlings.

Cheryl found that the life of the river and the life of the cottonwood are intimately connected. Disrupt one, and you disrupt the other.

The big streams that drain east from the Rockies into North America's Great Plains are volatile creatures. They flood each spring when the mountain snowpack melts and spring rains peak. By late May or early June, they are brown and ugly with runoff. Overflowing their banks, they spill into side channels and swales. Where water overflows or slows, silt settles out, enriching floodplain soils.

Along the main channel, the swollen river erodes the upstream sides of meander bends where the current is most powerful. The river balances its destructive work by depositing silt, sand and washed-out trees on the sheltered downstream sides of the bends, where the current is most gentle. Rivers like the Milk can rework their entire floodplains every decade or two.

Later in the summer, river flow drops to only a fraction of what it was during the spring flow. Through late summer and fall, the river depends on headwater forests that act as sponges, trapping rainfall and releasing it slowly into springs and creeks that sustain the shrunken river.

Cottonwoods set seed in June, when the spring runoff is at its peak. Billions of white, fluffy seeds set sail on the wind, drifting along the valleys until they find something damp to stick to. Many seeds eventually lodge at the edge of the flooding river on newly deposited point bars. There they sprout in a silty, well-watered seedbed.

Natural rivers follow much the same seasonal pattern of flood and ebb from year to year. The following June, consequent-

183

ly, usually brings a new layer of silt to bury the seedlings a little deeper. The flood waters also irrigate the young trees just when they need it most. If the river does not let them down for the first two or three years of life, the fast-growing young cottonwoods have no problem surviving.

Since the river reworks its floodplain annually, meanders migrate slowly down-valley over the passing years, as upstream edges wash out and downstream edges build up. The cottonwood forest migrates with the river. The youngest trees are always on the downstream sides of the bends, and the oldest on the upstream sides, where spring floods eventually washed them out.

Cottonwoods are becoming sparser along so many rivers from Alberta south to Texas because government water engineers have dammed most western rivers to regulate their flows.

A few foothills rivers, like the Highwood and the Belly, merely have diversion weirs that tilt some of the river's water into side valleys. However, large onstream dams plug the Red Deer, Bow, St. Mary's, Waterton and most other western rivers.

When water slows, it loses its ability to carry sand and silt. That is why rivers form deltas where they enter lakes and oceans. That is also why the reservoirs that form behind dams become giant silt traps during the muddy floods of springtime.

Cheryl Bradley and other researchers have found that downstream from dams, rivers cut down into the meanders they occupied before the dam's construction. Without the silt that it has lost to the bottom of the reservoir behind the dam, the river mines its own bed to restore its equilibrium. The meanders stop migrating and become entrenched. Cottonwood seeds, consequently, can no longer sprout on new point bars.

The water engineers who operate the dams use them to store spring flood waters. Again, this works against any young cottonwoods that manage to sprout downstream from the dam. Thirsty young seedlings can no longer rely on the spring floods as reliable sources of irrigation water.

New cottonwoods sprout too infrequently along the dammed, regulated rivers to keep pace with the death of the old trees.

That is what is happening along the Bow River today. Dr. Stewart Rood, a professor at the University of Lethbridge, has found a similar thing happening on the St. Mary's — which has lost more than half its cottonwoods since engineers dammed it in 1952 — and the Waterton River, which has lost a quarter of its cottonwoods since they dammed it in the 1960s.

The same thing will happen when Alberta Environment's water engineers finish building the notorious Oldman River Dam. This goes a long way in explaining the determination with which many Peigan Indians — whose reserve is downstream from the dam and to whom the cottonwood forests are sacred — continue their legal battle to have the dam shut down.

For anglers, however, maybe dams are not all bad. Admittedly, the eventual loss of cottonwoods might make the valley a little less scenic and a bit less pleasant on a hot summer's day. Perhaps those are small prices to pay, however, considering that dammed rivers control flows of water all year round. After all, the Bow River's Bearspaw Dam controls flows in the lower Bow. That flow control has played a big role in creating the internationally acclaimed lower Bow River fishery.

However, the cottonwood, the river and the trout are linked in more ways than one.

When cottonwoods turn golden and begin to shed their leaves in October, foothills and prairie rivers are at low ebb. Riffles are shallow and weak, backwaters flaccid; the rivers are sleepy.

Those same winds that spread cottonwood seeds in June still funnel down the valleys. Now, however, they pick up the golden wealth of thousands of big trees and whip the carbohydrate-rich leaves back and forth along the floodplain. Millions of dead leaves alight in the river, grow sodden, and sink.

Underwater, bacteria and fungus set to work decomposing the leaves. Beetle and caddis larvae munch away at the soggy harvest. Mayfly and stonefly nymphs feed on the smaller bits and the excretions of other invertebrates. Midge and blackfly larvae and net-spinning caddis filter bits of leaf debris out of the current. Willowfly and dragonfly nymphs hunt the river bed, preying on the leaf-eaters.

Whole guilds of insects rely on the leaf litter, processing and re-processing it as the seasons turn. Salmon flies grow large and protein-rich on organic detritus throughout the summer, fall and winter. When spring floods arrive to scour away the worked-over leaf litter, the salmonfly nymphs crawl ashore, hatch, and fly up…to shelter in the new year's crop of poplar leaves.

The river sustains the trees. The trees sustain the insect life. And the insect life sustains the trout.

Downstream from Calgary, the Bow River fishery will probably survive the depletion of that river's cottonwoods. The Bow has a substitute for poplar leaves; an entire city fertilizes the river with treated sewage.

But the lonely trout streams that drain the high plains — Willow Creek, the Oldman, Waterton and St. Mary's — have no such easy substitute. Their chief source of organic enrichment is their riparian mosaics of poplars, willows and other shrubbery. Those living mosaics rely on the natural rhythms of spring freshet and autumn drought to sustain them. And Alberta's water engineers have built lucrative careers out of rearranging those natural rhythms.

In the case of the Oldman River, the Alberta government has enlisted Stewart Rood to help them develop an operating plan for their new dam. They are counting on the plant ecologist's advice to help them save, or at least slow the loss of, the spectacular cottonwood forests all the way downstream to Lethbridge.

Rood hopes that the dam operators can sustain cottonwoods by releasing water in a way that mimics the spring flood, and by keeping the floodplain well-supplied with water all summer.

Cheryl Bradley is less optimistic. She points out that there is no way of restoring the silt and sediments trapped in the upstream reservoir. Without that sediment, the mock spring floods are more likely to scour out the river bed than to enrich the floodplain. Looking at the rivers that drain the high plains and foothills of the American West, where many dams have been in place for decades, ecologists see little cause for optimism. Most streams have lost, or are losing, much of their riparian forest.

Whatever the fate of the Oldman's floodplain forests, the controversy over the dam that threatens them offers a useful lesson. If we are to sustain the fisheries we have inherited, more by luck than by good planning, anglers must look beyond the trout and water engineers must look beyond the water. Those who wish to assert an unearned right to rearrange rivers would be wise to first learn to see the whole ecosystem in all its complexity — the subtle, intricate and inescapable connections among winds, and seasons, and floods, and trees, and soils, and leaves, and trout, and human decisions. It might temper their ambitions.

Certainly the seventeen-year-old angler fishing the darkened Bow River, while balsam poplars whispered in the wind and leaves floated past in the surface film, had no idea that those trees were anything more than scenery. He had no way of seeing that their leaves were anything other than a nuisance. He never suspected that those trees were not only part of his fishing experience but, ultimately, part of his river, and part of his fish.

He understands a little more now. And that understanding has raised a new and troubling question. To what extent will those trees be part of his future? ❧ *(1991)*

Leaning Upwind

Who Speaks for Running Waters?

I WENT DOWN TO THE BOW RIVER often during the strange evenings of my adolescence. It was a place where I could leave self-consciousness and tension behind. The sound of water lapping at the rounded cobbles was rhythmic, soothing and sure. Standing beside the evening river, I watched the rings of rising trout break the reflected light of street lamps.

"Who hears the rippling of rivers will not utterly despair of anything," Henry David Thoreau said. I think he was right. The Bow River helped me through many difficult times. That is the way it is with rivers, with clear flowing waters. They flow quietly through our lives, as constant and reassuring as the changing seasons or the ebb and flow of time.

One evening I drifted a muddler into an eddy at the tail of a long, quiet riffle and hooked a brown trout. The sun had set already. I had planned on this being my last cast but this was a big fish and he was not going to be hurried. He burrowed deep and stayed there, the powerful throbbing of his fight communicating itself up my line, through the rod, into my arm. The water was dark, full of quiet urgency as it slipped past and under the Crowchild bridge. I felt both fascinated by and fearful of the heavy thing alive at the end of my line, unseen beneath the river's flickering surface.

At length the fish turned into the main current, allowing the force of the river to help as it headed downstream, away from the pull. Unable to resist, I followed, obeying the pressure of fish and river, hands shaking at the thought of my leader separating. Its side broke the surface of the river and a tail splashed; then the fish was deep again, holding behind a slab of old sidewalk that city crews had dumped there. I held the pressure on. Nothing happened. The river lapped and chuckled as it always had, going somewhere else, letting me know that this was just between me and the fish.

More pressure, more resistance; then the fish gave a little. It was too dark to see into the water, but street light flickers showed the line of water behind my leader, and the bulges and swirls where the old trout struggled just below the surface. He ran again, held, then slid almost unresisting to the shallows where I dragged him, suddenly, from the secret water to the grass. Before he could flop back in, I pounced on him and subdued him with a stone.

The river flowed on through the night as I sat beside my victim and tried to fathom why I felt so moved by the night and the river and the trout that lay beside me in the grass, the chill of the water still on him.

That evening, in some way that I still cannot explain, remains in my memory as a pivotal event that helped me clarify my self, and my relation to the world. Perhaps it suffices to say that sometimes experience becomes parable. In any case, I can say now without embarrassment that I love the Bow River. It may seem a little alien: the thought of loving something you cannot hold, that is not human, that lacks the awareness to return that love. Yet I cannot look at the Bow River now without remembering countless things that, over the years, have become part of who I am. The late night struggle with the old brown trout. Evenings spent watching the passing water and wondering what was to become of my life. Canoeing in an October snowstorm with my wife-to-be. Obeying my two-year-old son's orders to bring him more rocks to throw.

Everyone has a river in their life. For me it was the Bow River, a few blocks from the family home in Calgary. For some friends of mine it is the Oldman, sliding peacefully past the garden their grandfather first dug sometime in the late 1800s. Kids dream dreams by their rivers. Fishermen cast flies upon them. Canoeists float along them. We build our homes near rivers. We walk with our lovers along their banks.

I remember canoeing the Oldman one day several years ago, slipping quietly from riffle to riffle as farms and river bottom pastures slid past. To me, this was all a new landscape; to others it was the home river, deeply familiar. I floated past buildings that had been put up a century ago, fences that showed signs of frequent repairs, old trees surrounding older houses, and pools where generations of anglers had fished. It occurred to me then that this river, which I was only discovering now for the first time, was part of the fabric and definition of countless people's lives. Farm kids had grown up here with the sounds and rhythms of the Oldman River worn deep into their hearts. Fishermen had developed that strange, jealous affection we all know so well for secret holes and favourite lies.

Every river in Alberta is like that. Each river has its own alumni whose lives will never be the same again, once the rhythm and magic of running waters have touched them.

Although we are a river people, the West's wealth is limited when it comes to rivers. Our rivers are the more precious and beautiful for their rarity. We don't need many to value them for what they are. As Roderick Haig-Brown said: "I have known very few rivers thoroughly and intimately. There is not time...."

My rivers are the Bow and the Oldman, the Maligne, Ram and Elbow, a few lesser streams, and that is all. My friends have their rivers. There are rivers I have never seen. They belong to others.

These are our rivers, and we are theirs. We can live away from them for long periods, just knowing they are there. Losing one, however, can feel like losing an arm, a child, or a much-loved parent.

The Oldman, for instance: the provincial government is

going to flood it. Many of us still cannot really come to terms with that idea. Miles of river will soon be gone, forever, always. The rest will change, its wild vitality replaced by calculated artifice as computers determine how much flow it will have from one day to the next.

A part of me, and a part of many other Albertans, will be lost when the Alberta government closes the gate on the Three Rivers Dam. Little pieces of countless peoples' lives died when the government filled the Dickson reservoir on the Red Deer, and the Bighorn reservoir on the North Saskatchewan. The Bow River may be dammed again soon. Each dam stops the laughter of the water, buries favourite trout pools, and erases the scenes and sounds that define somebody's memories of their life and home.

Rearranging Creation is easy when you see rivers as lines on maps, and consider them merely to be water resources. That is why the West's free flowing rivers are in trouble.

Damming rivers is sometimes presented as an essential matter of economics. The government's own numbers, however, have proved that the Dickson, Three Rivers and Milk River dams are all money-losers. Besides, money is not the issue. Our lives, and the quality of our lives, is what our rivers are all about.

It is our government that is building the Three Rivers Dam on the Oldman. In a democratic country, we elect governments to help arrange society in the ways that best satisfy our idea of a fair and rational civilization. Governments change as our needs and values change because they know they must respond to our wishes if they hope to survive. That is the theory.

A democratic government exists to serve the people who elect it. So how does the resignation with which we sit back and let economists and politicians who know little about the real value of our rivers build dams and reservoirs we neither want nor need, relate to our privilege of living in a democratic society?

I don't know. I do know that when the part of me that is the Oldman River disappears at last beneath the muddy waters of a wind-scoured irrigation reservoir, I will be a little less whole. The province of my birth will be a little less like home. I also know that I will have gone down kicking. The government has no doubts about where I stand; many of my letters reside in their files.

I guess few others bothered writing. The dam is going up.

I once heard that politicians work on the basis that one letter represents the wishes of a thousand voters. When I contemplate the fact that Alberta's living rivers are at the heart of what makes our lives rich, and that the sound of running water echoes in the hearts of we who have chosen to make our homes here, I cannot help feeling that we have failed ourselves. I remember the words of British Columbia poet Dale Zieroth, anguished over the possible fate of his own home river, the upper Columbia:

...And when I ask you
where are your friends
there is only silence.
It is the sound of the mountains coming down
with their creeks, coming down through the ice.
It is the sound of men fighting, men
failing to fight, and men
passing.... ✣ *(1986)*

Of Wave Pools and Stream "Enhancement"

KAYAKERS LOVE THE GIANT wave pool at West Edmonton Mall. Every several minutes it creates the perfect wave, a predictable environment they can use to hone their paddling skills. On the Kananaskis River, whitewater freaks plan their trips around scheduled releases of water from the hydropower plants upstream. To make kayaking more fun, the power company has installed boulders at strategic spots: perfect, predictable eddies.

In a similar way, children love the Allan Bill fishing pond. It is an artificial impoundment at the bottom of a former gravel quarry. Fisheries trucks periodically stock the pond with hatchery rainbows of catchable size. All children need to do is throw in a hook with a miniature marshmallow. Eventually a bewildered little trout will try to eat it.

Alberta's pheasant population crashed in the late 1960s, the result of continuing habitat loss and two bad winters in a row. In the wake of the crash, many hunters were thrilled to learn that Alberta Fish and Wildlife was going to expand their pheasant hatchery. I still remember the first time I encountered the new hatchery pheasants. Five confused little cock pheasants stepped out in front of our car. Dad had nearly to kick one to get them to fly. That day, we all went home with our limit of pheasants. We should have been delighted, but we felt vaguely ashamed.

That was the first time I began seriously to consider the consequences of replacing the wild and unpredictable with the artificial and trivial, in the name of better recreation.

Last June I travelled to southwestern Alberta to fish the Crowsnest River's stonefly hatch with an old friend, Dave Soltess. In the backseat I had a newly minted copy of Alberta Environment's final mitigation plan for the Three Rivers Dam, which will destroy the most productive reaches of the Crowsnest and Oldman Rivers.

While there, we checked out some experimental mitigation works already installed. Perfectly placed midstream boulders guarantee just the right number of holding spots on long riffles. Mitigation engineers have buried precast concrete overhangs at stream bends to provide hiding spots that will not wash out. Symmetrical weirs and deflection devices channel the river flow into deep pools.

According to the plan, Alberta Environment will thus improve much of the upper Crowsnest, to ensure "no net loss of recreational fishing opportunity." It is a fine trout stream, but we have the technology to make it even better.

The Castle, another river that the dam will flood, has fine trout habitat, too. Its trout don't grow as large or abundant as those in the Crowsnest, however. The mitigation folks suspect that the stream needs more organic matter. They plan to enhance the Castle River fishery by fertilizing it. They have not said, yet, what sort of nutrient enrichment they are planning — perhaps a feedlot or two?

A disturbing thread runs through all the examples cited above. All offer the same easy sort of seduction to which many recreationists readily succumb. Anglers are just as vulnerable as anyone else — perhaps more so. Stepping back once in a while to reevaluate our motives may be worthwhile. It can help ensure we are not chasing solutions to the wrong problems, at the risk of making things worse.

Aldo Leopold, more than fifty years ago, wrote: "All intergrades of artificiality exist, but as mass-use increases it tends to push the whole gamut of conservation techniques toward the artificial end, and the whole scale of trophy values downward." I have no doubt that he, like Dave or me, would have enjoyed hooking a four-pound brown from beneath one of the concrete overhangs on the Crowsnest. I suspect that he, too, would have felt the same nagging sense of loss.

Wild streams, wild trout and wild places were still abundant in Leopold's time, but even then he saw that some things were going awry. Leopold tried to define what outdoors people want from fish, wildlife and habitat management. He asked what we really seek when we go down to the river.

In part, he concluded, we go to rediscover our heritage, leaving the here-and-now behind while we return to the landscapes and experiences that gave shape to our cultural identity. This is a powerful force still. Tradition and nostalgia figure strongly in many of our choices. Arguably, as traces of the natural landscape that shaped our culture become fewer and further between, the drive to return to the primitive will grow even stronger.

In part, Leopold suspected, we seek out activities that will strengthen our bond to the land that sustains us. In an urbanized, consumptive society convincing ourselves that we are somehow exempt from the complex webs of ecological relationships that define land can be too easy. Lurking in our psyche there is a powerful need to reestablish links: to become a part of the natural world and restore our balance. Go to the river, immerse yourself in water-noise and leaf-shadow; the land begins to seep back into your being.

The third value that Leopold felt outdoors people derive from sports like angling was the ethical value of indulging in an activity that demands moral restraint and self-control. In his day, catch-and-release fishing was something anglers did only when their creel was full. I suspect he would be pleased to see the extent to which it has come to define many anglers' idea of an ethical approach to fishing.

Leopold stopped at three primary values of outdoor recreation. In doing so, I think he missed one of the most important values we derive from fishing. At best, he touched upon it only tangentially.

Society expends a great deal of effort on creating stable, predictable environments. We chafe at power failures, because they interrupt so many electronic rituals that make our lives predictable. If the snowplough does not clear the roads quickly, we protest angrily. We do not like people to be late. We resent unexpected callers.

For each degree of success in controlling our environment, I believe our nature demands more randomness and risk. Perhaps this relates to our ecological roots as part of living nature. In nature we are only part of a vast web of interconnected forces, creatures, plants and events. When we dominate the environment and establish the predictability we think we want, we lose that perspective. But wading belly-deep in a powerful foothills river, surrounded with space and birdsong and the scent of wolf willow and rose, unsure where the fish are and if our lure will attract them, contemplating the possibility of bears, drowning or simply getting lost — we are back in the real world. All guarantees are off. Anything is possible.

How does this relate to wave pools and concrete overhangs?

To quote Leopold again, "Bigger and better gadgets are good for industry, so why not for outdoor recreation? It has not dawned on [recreationists] that outdoor recreations are essentially primitive, atavistic; that their value is a contrast-value; that excessive mechanization destroys contrast by moving the factory to the woods or to the marsh."

Roderick Haig-Brown, Canada's greatest angling writer, agreed. "It is difficult to describe what I mean by 'quality fishing'…. It is fishing that sets problems and allows for, even demands, skillful performance; it implies preservation, so far as possible, of natural conditions in the waters, their surroundings and the fish themselves...it is fishing where unexpected things can and do happen, fishing where a man has room to move and think and see and hear and be himself."

No natural stream will support as many fish as it might, simply because no natural stream functions primarily as a habitat for trout. An angler might be excused for assuming otherwise, but streams exist to support not only trout but suckers, leeches, algae, willows, bacteria, deer, evaporation, sandpipers and snakes. A stream with just the right proportion of riffles to pools and of undercuts to rills exists only in the textbook and the fancy of the trout fisher. In real life, streams are complex, frustrating, unpredictable, and imperfect.

That is how it should be. Because that is what we need, although it might not seem obvious when we are untangling our backcast from yet another alder.

I remember reading a short story, years ago, in which an angler died and went — he thought — to heaven. There he was outfitted with beautiful gear and turned out onto a pool in a perfect spring stream. He cast flawlessly and hooked a fine trout right where he knew it should be. Then he cast and caught another in the same spot. Only after several perfect casts and perfect trout did the truth dawn on him — his was an eternal curse, not an eternal reward!

The more we artificialize the environment to increase its ability to produce fish or game, the more we cheat ourselves. Anglers or hunters who — lacking serious reflection — measure success by fish hooked or animals bagged, risk blindly accepting the ongoing degradation of the essential values of their sports. Deer hunters too often applaud when they hear of predator-control programs, logging activity, Bucks-for-Wildlife alfalfa plantings and other programs that seem likely to ensure more deer to be shot. Anglers too, have shown a fine enthusiasm for fish stocking, artificial impoundments and — more recently — stream "enhancements."

Not long ago I read about some of the Bow River Chapter of Trout Unlimited Canada's recent habitat improvement projects. Included in the list was a project to dynamite a passage around a waterfall on Trap Creek. Blasting the falls would enable spawning Bow River rainbows to travel further upstream. Something about that project troubled me. I know now what it was.

Trap Creek is a natural stream. It is the native habitat of the west-slope cutthroat, a fish that has suffered badly from genetic pollution. Throughout most of its natural range, the cutthroat has hybridized with introduced rainbows. The waterfall was a natural waterfall. It was the predictable result of what happens when a foothills stream encounters an up-tilted bed of the Paskapoo sandstone that underlies, and helps define, the foothills landscape. It was part of both the stream and the landscape.

Unlike other stream projects that repair damage caused by overgrazing, highway construction, coal mining, resource development and other forms of modern industrial development, this was an attempt to improve on Nature. What the project really achieved was to replace a relatively natural stream, and a relatively natural fauna, with one artificialized to produce more fish. It seemed like such a good idea, but this project violated all three of the values Aldo Leopold identified as central to the sport of angling.

One step closer to the wave pool.... Over the last century, Canadians have built one of the wealthiest countries on the globe. We did it, for the most part, by aggressively exploiting this land's natural wealth. We could have done it differently. We could have chosen restraint, treating the land and its streams with sensitivity, but we opted for rapid growth and easy wealth. Because of our haste and greed, the land has been left with a legacy of sick and wounded watercourses.

Trout Unlimited and other conservation groups have done much good in trying to atone for past excesses, by restoring productivity to ruined streams. The successes have been gratifying — true sources of hope and inspiration. But are we really clear on our underlying philosophy?

Are we clearly focused on ecological restoration, or do we risk letting our zeal to improve streams become yet another form of exploitation?

In the frontier tradition, are we willing to sacrifice wildness and unpredictability — values of no apparent benefit to ourselves — to produce more and larger fish? Or are we mature enough to recognize that the stream is much more than its water, its trout, or the sublime delights of catching and releasing big fish — and that neither we nor any other interest group has an inherent right to rearrange a healthy stream for our own purposes?

To repair a wounded stream is an act of atonement, an acknowledgement of responsibility: good stewardship. To "improve" a healthy stream that happens not to hold as many fish as we would like, however, risks being an act of arrogance, little different from exploiting it for any other narrow purpose. In the old days we increased a stream's trout-holding capacity by treating it with rotenone to remove fish we considered undesirable competition. Few would countenance this kind of violence now. Today, however, we appear willing to watch the Crowsnest River fitted with engineering marvels that will increase the number of trout at the expense of other species' habitat. Is there really that much difference between the two approaches?

Twenty years ago, in his great book *Fisherman's Summer*, Roderick Haig-Brown prescribed an ethic for those who value streams and fishing, and wish to ensure that both will survive into the future: "Many waters still provide quality fishing without the slightest aid or interference from man; it is important to preserve these. Many waters would still provide quality fishing but for the interference or mismanagement of man; it is important to restore these."

We have the technology to ruin streams. We have the technology to "enhance" them. But do we have the humility and wisdom to protect dynamic, healthy, imperfect streams from our own zeal? ❧ *(1988)*

A Plague of Roads

MY FIRST ELK WAS ON THE WRONG side of a big mountain.
Actually, it was on the summit ridge. At the shot, however, it bolted straight down the slope and into the timber. It only collapsed when it had run downhill at least two hundred vertical feet.

This was my first elk, as I said. Until a hunter gets that first one, elk are more theoretical than real. When I walked up to that huge, six-point bull, however, abstract notion became sobering reality. You can wrestle a whitetail buck over a high ridge. With a bull elk, simply gutting the animal is more work than most of us do in a week. Moving it single-handedly is hopeless.

I was a lot wiser, and poorer, by midafternoon of the following day. The two young horse-packers I had finally tracked down after several phone calls off-loaded my quartered prey beside my car, pocketed their profit, and headed home. These days I still prowl the far country in my quest for elk. Unless I am within a mile of a road when I find them, however, with no intervening mountaintops, I leave my rifle slung on my shoulder.

This is not that difficult. There are roads everywhere, it seems: a veritable plague of roads.

More roads than elk.

Elk, for the first half of the twentieth century, were beyond the reach of most hunters. Few Albertans were fortunate enough to live in elk country. Elk hunting, for the most part, was a privilege reserved for wealthy easterners who could afford to travel by train to western Canada and pay outfitters to pack them into the wilderness.

Since the 1920s, however, roads have gradually penetrated deep into the backcountry, fanning up the side valleys and over the ridges. Some were built for logging, some for mining and many, in my home ground of western Alberta, to explore for oil and gas. One way or another, taxpayers footed the bills for most of them. Government agencies consequently adopted the philosophy that citizens should be able to enjoy those roads. It looked better, politically, than restricting access to the resource companies whose sophisticated lobbying got the things built in the first place.

So it goes. It is getting hard to be alone with an elk in today's West. For the price of a tank of gas, just about anyone who wants can race you to it.

As early as 1940, Aldo Leopold warned that the exponential growth in roads may not be an unmixed blessing for hunters and anglers. "Recreational development," he wrote, "is a job not of building roads into lovely country, but of building receptivity into the still unlovely human mind."

In the 1960s and 1970s, the oil and gas industry ruled Alberta. Few people seriously considered suggesting they should not carve roads into the last hidden corners of the province. Many of us took advantage of those new roads to get within walking distance of creeks and rivers that had previously only been squiggly lines on maps. The fishing, often as not, was fantastic…at least for the first few years.

"Many of those headwater creeks," fisheries biologist Carl Hunt told me, years later, "have very limited productivity. Winters are long, summers are cool, and the streams are small. In their pristine state, they had healthy populations of good-sized fish, but once those were fished out the streams didn't recover."

Fisheries managers have been forced to bring in increasingly restrictive size and catch limits. Tougher restrictions reduce the fish kill closer to what it might be in streams with poorer road access. You cannot have wilderness-quality fishing if there is a road along the creek; it's that simple.

Caribou, elk and other large animals also suffered from the growing network of woods roads.

The highway and railroad to Grande Cache, constructed in the 1960s, delivered a double-whammy to caribou. Trains and cars slaughtered many of these naive, wilderness animals, especially in winter when road salt attracts ungulates onto the highway. Once-remote populations in the Willmore and Simonette country also became readily accessible to hunters as new resource roads fanned out from the highway corridor.

Caribou are ridiculously easy to hunt, and breed at a far slower rate than moose or deer. The upshot: there no longer is a hunting season for caribou in Alberta. The government classifies them as a threatened species, thanks largely to the enlightened lobbying of the Alberta Fish and Game Association. But the road network continues to spread as resource industries exploit the north country. Caribou may be safe from hunters, but growing numbers continue to die in collisions and at the hands of vandals.

Researchers in the western states have found that hunted elk develop a habit of avoiding roads because of their high sensitivity to human activity. Elk rarely use many seemingly ideal habitats dissected by high densities of back roads. Biologists use the term "habitat effectiveness" to describe this phenomenon. Habitat may look good, but it is not effective if animals will not or cannot use it.

Based on this research, biologists now estimate that every mile of road per square mile of forested elk habitat translates into a 25 percent loss of elk habitat, because of reduced habitat effectiveness. In more open countryside, this increases to 50 percent. Researchers have determined that up to 70 percent of elk habitat in southwestern Alberta's Castle and Carbondale River valleys has been lost because of the density of roads in that area. Game surveys support this conclusion. In the 1950s the area supported more than three thousand elk. Today it holds fewer than twelve hundred.

Elk hunters may like roads that penetrate deep into elk country — but because of those roads, they find fewer elk. You cannot, it appears, have it both ways.

B.C.'s Ministries of Forests and of Environment recognize the problem. They have instituted seasonal road closures that restrict sport hunters from using logging roads in critical wildlife areas. Most of the closures are on the honour system, however. Poachers have no honour, so the closures do little to improve habitat effectiveness. They only reduce access for legitimate hunters.

A couple of years ago, I was shocked to learn that Alberta Fish and Wildlife had designated my favourite whitetail hunting area near Hinton, Alberta as a wildlife sanctuary. I can no longer hunt there, although the Camp 1 area teems with whitetails.

The sanctuary, the local wildlife officers explained to me, was the only effective way to reestablish an elk population in what should be ideal habitat. Natives exercising their legitimate Treaty hunting rights had been using the spiderweb network of back roads throughout the area so effectively that they killed more elk than were born to replace the losses. When wildlife authorities proposed simply to close the roads, local recreationists angrily insisted that they have a right to play on those roads with their off-road vehicles.

The only way to keep the roads and restore the elk was to establish a wildlife sanctuary.

Now, nobody can hunt there. Another area is out of bounds.

Nobody can hunt in most of the Kananaskis valley either. The narrow dirt road my grandfather drove when he hunted there years ago is now a paved highway. Many urban recreationists now use the highway. Most do not like the sound of gunshots and the sight of gut piles. The solution: close the hunting season.

At first glance, a new road would seem to be good news to hunters who want to get a little deeper into the backcountry. Once the road is there, however, by definition the backcountry is not. If hunting — real hunting for healthy populations of wild animals in natural settings — is going to survive, it will survive longer in the backcountry where there are no road hunters, few urban recreationists, and little hunting pressure.

"To build a road is so much simpler than to think of what the country really needs," Aldo Leopold wrote, half a century ago.

What the country really needs is for a whole lot of roads to be put to bed and reclaimed. Only by closing roads will we restore the wildness that is at the heart of truly great hunting and fishing experiences. ❧ *(1993)*

Have Our National Parks Failed Us?

JUST EAST OF BANFF NATIONAL PARK, the Trans-Canada Highway bulges into a six-lane freeway. Entrances and exits spin off in all directions. Street lamps line the pavement, illuminating the surge and flow of tourists shuttling between Calgary and Banff.

South of the highway is Canmore, a sprawling community of old coal miners' homes and new condominiums, national park employees and real estate speculators. Pervading the clear mountain air that whistles down the streets of Canmore, like a vision of wealth and fame, is the rumour of the 1988 Winter Olympics. Developers, with government money, are building a new ski resort on Mount Allan, a few miles away. Everyone's home has become an investment.

North of the highway, the mountains swell up and away. These are the Front Ranges of the Rockies, a dry, wind-blown sort of mountains whose grassy slopes alternate with gullies full of aspens and glacial terraces clothed in lodgepole pine and Douglas fir. The winter snow that falls here is blown away by Chinook winds even while the surrounding mountains remain deep in snow. It is an excellent place: a spectacular mosaic of vegetation, rock and wind, a haven for wildlife, and the scenic backdrop that gives the area its appeal to visitors.

Mule deer and elk rely on these slopes for winter feed. Many animals come from Banff National Park, unaware of having crossed the boundary lines. They come here because the snow is shallow and feed is abundant. Bighorn sheep cluster on the higher slopes. Black bears den in the wooded gullies. Overhead, eagles soar.

It is a place well-loved by people, too. On any weekend day many people stroll, hike, or lounge about enjoying the scenery. Riders follow horse trails along the ridges. Children from town cross the highway and head up on the slopes in search of adventure. People scramble to the mountaintops.

Others calculate how much the view will be worth when the Olympic boom hits. They survey roads. They subdivide. They speculate.

One September day a couple of years ago, my wife and I took a walk in the aspens to watch autumn blaze across the valley. We saw an eagle, seven mule deer, a herd of bighorn sheep, two horseback riders, and a large bulldozed swath. Survey markers spread beyond into the forest; it was the beginning of a housing subdivision.

The new subdivision's name, appropriately, is Elk Run.

The sight of a bulldozer scar on an unspoiled slope — of survey stakes next to piles of deer droppings — troubled us and spoiled the pleasure of the day. It seemed violent and amoral to strip off the soil and bury the crocuses, rose tangles, wildlife winter range and scenery, in order to build luxury second homes that will stand empty for much of each year.

My disillusionment grew, however, when I mentioned the destruction to a Canmore resident, a naturalist who has fought long and hard to limit development in Banff National Park. His response: "Well, I find it hard to get too upset about it. For one thing, it's not in the park. For another thing, it is zoned for municipal development."

His response struck a discordant note. On reflection, I realized the underlying meaning of his response: our national parks, wilderness areas and other protected areas have failed us, in a very basic and vital way.

They have not drawn us into a more thoughtful relationship with our habitat. They have not taught us that we should use land frugally, and with humility and respect. They have encouraged us to embrace an approach to conservation that consists mostly of trading large protected areas in exchange for freedom to abuse all other land.

They have more than failed. They have become a symptom of the problem.

In 1949 the American conservationist Aldo Leopold published his now-famous argument for the development of a land ethic. He said that we were all members of a biotic community. As such, we should afford to the land the same ethical responsibility and restraint with which we strive to treat our fellow man. He argued that a sense of stewardship, or husbandry, should guide land use decisions.

In the four decades since, we cannot say that land use decisions have become any simpler, nor that they have come to be informed by a spirit of ethical restraint. Against the complex realities of a shrinking world, growing populations, increasing technology and spreading urbanization, it has become too easy for those who care about land to taste despair, and fall back into a siege mentality.

If we cannot treat all land responsibly, this point of view argues, let's settle for protecting some patches from the despoilers.

As the destructive potential of man increased in the postwar years, so did the concern of those who saw that potential applied to land. The forces became increasingly polarized. Somehow, the term "conservation" became replaced by "preservation" in the frequent confrontations between developers and environmentalists. Distrust on both sides has created a rhetorical war of issues, rather than a dialectic exchange of values and understanding. In the determination of both sides to establish and defend precedents, the important questions go unasked. Real communication goes begging.

In a national park one is not allowed to pick a flower. One is discouraged from — and could be fined for — eating a berry. One must stay on the trail. The many shalt-nots are understandable because of the popularity of national parks. Parks staff speak of the danger of loving a park to death. Five hundred people a day could trample a mountain meadow to mud in a week.

But the unfortunate corollary of these restrictions is that they perpetuate the myth that humans and nature are not part of the same thing — that man is not a full member of the biotic community. National parks do not bring people nearer to nature; on the contrary, their experiences there too often reinforce the idea that they are outsiders. By extension, park visitors are encouraged to believe that outside the parks, in those unfortunate places that do not enjoy protection from the inevitably destructive choices of we outsiders, nature must be — at least usually — written off.

Destructive development? Irresponsible land use? That is the nature of the beast, we assume. Thank God at least that we have our national parks.

The irony of this paradox becomes apparent when we examine tradeoffs we have accepted, to save national parks from despoliation.

The Calgary Olympic Development Association (CODA) campaigned aggressively, and successfully, to have the International Olympic Commission (IOC) designate Calgary as the site of the 1988 Winter Olympics. One keystone of CODA's bid was Mount Sparrowhawk, south of Canmore. The Olympic promoters touted the windswept mountain as the ideal race site for the Men's Downhill skiing.

No sooner had the IOC approved Calgary's bid than disturbing rumours began to appear in the press. Nancy Greene Rainier stated that Sparrowhawk was the wrong choice. Others said it would not hold snow. The mutter of rumours swelled. Lobbyists suggested other choices. Two years later the Alberta government announced its final site selection. Mount Allan, a few miles east, would be the Olympic ski area.

Mount Allan differs from Mount Sparrowhawk in having less snow-holding ability, little suitable racing terrain, and one of the world's largest and healthiest herds of bighorn sheep.

Forty miles west, in Banff National Park, is the sprawling downhill ski complex of Lake Louise. The area was the subject of repeated controversy and a stormy series of public hearings in 1972 when Parks Canada and Imperial Oil Ltd. jointly proposed a major expansion. Ever since public opinion saved the Lake Louise area from Imperial Oil (but not from Parks Canada, which incrementally developed the area anyway) environmental organizations have guarded the area jealously, if less than effectively.

With the first suggestion that Mount Sparrowhawk might be unacceptable, the watchdog organizations pricked up their ears. Could this be a new conspiracy to expand Lake Louise, they wondered? Perhaps CODA intended to use Lake Louise all along but had used the Sparrowhawk option, outside the national park, to win the IOC's approval. The government's subsequent selection of Mount Allan, an obviously unsuitable mountain, only served to deepen suspicions.

CODA denied all rumours. The environmental groups eased into the firing line, just in case.

The ski development at Lake Louise has been in existence for many years already, and has almost doubled in size since 1972. In spite of the National Parks Act, the area is far from unspoiled. It is in deep snow country in the central Rockies, too far west to sustain wintering populations of ungulates. It is within bus and train distance of Canmore and Banff, and already has parking facilities and other infrastructure.

It might have been argued that the Men's Downhill at Lake Louise would be unlikely to degrade so heavily developed

212

an area further. It might have been argued that the undisturbed slopes of Mount Allan had higher and better uses than ski development. It certainly should have been argued that an ethical attitude to all land would favour the concentration of facilities, as much as possible, in areas already developed.

Those points might have been argued, but they were not.

Lake Louise is in a national park. Mount Allan is not. National parks are sacrosanct. We can sacrifice Mount Allan.

Mount Allan's fate suggests that we have cheated ourselves, with our penchant for easy either/or decisions. We chose a simple, rational approach to conservation that, in the end, continues to work against conservation. We opted to draw lines on maps, zoning one area for preservation, another for development, another for exploitation. Somehow, we convinced ourselves that this is a responsible approach to conservation.

We have taken the easy road of trying to protect artificial units of land — making them somehow more valuable than other land, however similar. The more difficult road remains little travelled. It would require that we educate ourselves and others to see land as an extension of ourselves that we should use wisely and conservatively. All land.

It is the nature of regulations that they live only so long. Then they are amended or abandoned. Lake Louise will continue to develop and expand. So will Canmore and — now — Mount Allan. People will flock to the national parks where earnest staff will urge them to stay on trails and not pick berries. Environmental groups will fight to preserve more land, and developers will rage about elitism and resource lockups.

And we will continue to wonder why, with so much seemingly sincere concern about our environment, so many people continue to be misuse, abuse, and put it to all the wrong kinds of uses.

Somewhere along the road to sustainability, we took a wrong turn. It happened when we institutionalized and segregated both conservation and resource development. Rather than creatively bringing the two together in the context of a land ethic — in an environment of mutual education and an atmosphere of good faith — we chose to isolate them by drawing arbitrary lines on maps and laws on paper. Lines and laws can be — and are constantly — amended. Only an ethic has lasting survival value.

If this were a perfect world and humans viewed themselves as citizens of their habitat, we would not need national parks. The very notion of national parks would be absurd.

However, this is not a perfect world. In too many cases, we have chosen to make it a world where setting aside national parks and protected areas substitutes for ethical restraint and hard choices. We have traded our responsibility toward the land for a few small museum-pieces that must always remain more a symptom of our affliction, than a cure for our ills. ❧ *(1986)*

Violence at Mountain Park

I USED TO HIKE UP THROUGH resin-scented forests south of Hinton to hunt bighorn sheep among the mountaintops.

I remember climbing out of predawn mist one day onto the open slopes of Prospect Mountain and seeing the world turn gold as the rising sun burned off the valley fog. Below lay a tapestry of green pine forest, golden shrub meadows where elk fed quietly, talus slopes, and bogs. A thin grey ribbon marked the road from Cadomin to the Cardinal River Divide.

As I had often before, I studied this wild Alberta landscape with the same aching pleasure I feel while watching the sleeping face of the wife I love. I felt rich beyond all hope.

Sitting by a streamside meadow to eat lunch, the intricacy of the vegetation struck me at close range. Wheatgrasses, pussytoes, louseworts and countless other native plants mingled in a dense, continuous mosaic of spruce forest, sedge meadow, alder thicket and aspen bluff.

Generations of weasels had hunted generations of mice amidst that living tapestry. Moose wandered from willow tangle to aspen bluff, wolves travelled the ridges, flocks of redpolls descended in enthusiastic chaos into the birches — sometimes the landscape seemed to teem with life. Other times it seemed lifeless, as still as the cold cliffs.

Picking my way along the sheep trails, I sometimes felt like an outsider. I wanted to be part of all this; I studied to belong, but in the evenings I went home. That worked against me. Still, I persevered.

One day I did get a sheep. Leaving the entrails for the ravens who watch over this country, I loaded the meat into my pack. Having been awake and working hard since before dawn, I decided to rest awhile. I fell asleep watching ravens circle above the ridge.

Later I woke, fought the pack onto my shoulders, stood up...and there were grizzly tracks. I had slept, with a pack full of meat, beside his hours-old spoor. It was a reminder that in this sort of country, human beings are among the lesser creatures. Chastened, grateful for the reprieve, I headed home.

The road home cut through big strip mines where overfed bighorn sheep watched from the roadsides, complacent as cows and not much brighter. The coal companies really like those sheep feeding on the alfalfa they have planted on their slack heaps. See? Strip mining is green.

215

But there is no sense of history or place in those minescapes. The sheep are tame. There is no great bear. There is nothing to which a human being can ache to belong.

Now Cheviot Mines wants to strip coal from under the Mountain Park country, right to the edge of Jasper National Park. When they are finished, there will be a few hundred square kilometres more of alfalfa, rubble, bighorns, and little else. Investors will pocket their profits and move on.

That humans can still seriously contemplate violence on this scale is, I believe, deeply frightening. It implies a fundamental moral deadness: a vast dysfunction.

Some argue that Hinton needs the strip-mining jobs so that young families will not have to move to find work. Mine jobs pay well. Good people work there. What else are we going to do now that the frontier is gone?

Swan Hills got its toxic waste treatment plant and Pincher Creek its mud-encrusted Oldman River Dam because of those sorts of arguments. These are frightened arguments founded not on love of place or integrity of vision but on a collective inability to see beyond the near abyss. Just give me a few more good years until this mine runs out, the logic goes; somebody will come up with something sustainable in the meantime.

And if they do not, what are we left with? Ravaged landscapes, no pride, no jobs.

Stripping the life from that Mountain Park country, I would argue, should be an act of desperation. Surely this is something a society that identifies itself with its land would consider only as a last resort: like burning the furniture to keep warm.

Lately I have wondered if this time I should just go stand in front of the bulldozers.

I will not, of course: we Albertans are a conservative

216

bunch who tend to view that sort of thing as a radical act. Most of us, however, do not consider it radical for a transnational corporation to strip the life, history and meaning from an ancient, healthy landscape, in order to export a dirty fuel to an overpopulated nation. ॐ *(1997)*

Coming Home

Better Anthropocentrism

WHAT A MESS WE HAVE MADE of things.

There are those who say that the human species is a failed experiment, an animal whose uniquely conscious intelligence is less a blessing than a fatal curse. Our consciousness is unprecedented in the living world, yet it too readily manifests itself as a self-centredness that pollutes, degrades, exploits and destroys the natural environment.

Others say there is still hope, if we can eliminate anthropocentricity — our traditional focus on the needs, wants, and self-interest of the human animal. Instead, they say, we need to develop an ethic that places the good of the ecosystem, of the biosphere, above the self-interest of people. Ecologist Stan Rowe describes such an ethic as biocentrism, or ecocentrism.

There can be no question that we need to motivate ourselves to act in ways that sustain ecosystems at the expense of our own comforts and short-term wants. Yet the idea that we can do this by substituting ecocentrism for anthropocentrism, I believe, is flawed both logically and ecologically.

Dr. Rowe argues that humans have become too isolated from nature. By differentiating between anthropocentricity and ecocentricity, however, he implicitly supports the idea that humankind is separate from nature.

Saying that everything is at the centre of the universe might be closer to the truth. To a giant liver fluke — a translucent parasite that lives inside elk livers — the universe exists to serve giant liver flukes. To a limestone rock, the universe exists to create limestone rocks. To a human being, the universe exists for humans to use.

Every one of these perspectives is true, and provable.

221

That is the nature of life: a web of relationships and consequence ultimately connects all things. For that reason, we can prove that all things exist to serve the needs of any single thing that we choose to look at in isolation. This is not wrong. In fact, it may hold the key to resolving the problem of environmental degradation caused by human species-selfishness.

One test of any premise's validity is one's gut reaction to it: does it feel right? Arguing that humans must become less anthropocentric feels wrong, because it proposes to deny a fundamental principle of ecology. In a functioning ecosystem, each organism or entity acts — to the extent that it can act — in the interests of its self and its family. The remarkable thing about ecosystems is that they integrate the self-interest of a vast diversity of living things into a greater, interdependent whole. What might seem to be destructive self-centredness for each individual animal or plant, ultimately strengthens and sustains the ecosystem.

A coyote kills other animals to sustain its own life. Other animals flee and hide from the coyote to sustain their own lives. The interaction strengthens both, by selecting for the most effective predator and the most effective prey. Predation — the ongoing conflict between competing self-interests — thus becomes a cooperative function. It is good for both hunter and hunted and, by extension, for the ecosystem of which they are elements.

The human conundrum is that our species' self-interest is out of whack. Ever more of what we do disrupts, degrades and harms the ecosystems of which we are elements, rather than strengthening them.

This is why Stan Rowe and other thoughtful ecologists argue that we need to become less self-centred (anthropocentric) and more focused on the needs of ecological systems and the ecosphere as a whole (ecocentric).

This is correct as far as it goes. The problem is, it just will not work. Self interest is an ecological *sine qua non*. We cannot just turn it off.

If nature demands that we be self-interested, then, I suspect that what we need is a better definition of self.

What is a species?

I recall visiting the Calgary Zoo one day with the family. The children wanted to look at animals. A massive Siberian tiger overwhelmed them with its tiger-ness. It was a magnificent specimen in a large open air enclosure where it could exercise, find privacy, stalk passers by and live a generally satisfactory existence — certainly as good as any zoo tiger could enjoy.

Nevertheless, this tiger had never stalked and killed a wild deer. It had never waded a reedgrass swamp or smelled the resin-scented wind sweeping in off the Aldan Plateau. The grass it bedded down in was Kentucky bluegrass, a tame hay species. The trees that shaded it were black poplars, endemic to North America. It had been born in a zoo, grown to maturity and would die in a zoo without ever killing a thing.

Was this a tiger? Is a species merely the sum of its chromosomes translated into a certain shape and pattern? Is that all there is to being a tiger?

A tiger without its habitat, I submit, is no tiger at all. It is merely a convincing facsimile. If the native habitat of the tiger is gone, then the tiger is gone too because there can never again be a real tiger. A real tiger is potential interacting with context over time. In fact, that is a reasonable definition for any individual. In the zoo, the context is not tiger context; thus, the individual becomes something less than a tiger.

Hatchery trout also illustrate this point. Long ago, fish culturists removed rainbow trout from stream ecosystems. Generations of trout had hatched and died in those ecosystems. Natural selection had fitted those fish to the seasonal cycles of their streams, and to the other animals that shared those ecosystems. The wild fish had spawned, fed and sheltered within the all-encompassing, unique and dynamic ecosystem of which they were a part.

Reared in hatcheries, the descendants of those trout continued to look like rainbow trout. However, through generations of crowded captive breeding under controlled conditions, they developed a tendency to feed aggressively, cluster in large groups, and take shelter in open water rather than under cover. This fitted their new context: the hatchery pond. They no longer needed to maintain their stock knowledge of flood cycles, predators and disease. They had become convincing counterfeits.

When fisheries managers stocked hatchery fish into the same streams where their ancestors had lived, they did not fit. They no longer were rainbow trout, in other words; they were hatchery trout. The stocked fish instinctively behaved in ways that had always worked before. Behaviour that had served them well in fish tanks, however, worked against their survival in natural streams. The trout had lost touch with the natural ecosystems in which their identity resided.

The same principles hold true for humans. Complex brains and opposable thumbs aside, we are animals subject to the same natural laws that govern other animals. By definition, then, we are ecological beings: products of and, ultimately, parts of greater ecosystems. Can one be a human being without context, or is one just unfulfilled potential and maladaptation?

Some of our most powerful and poignant literature is rooted in other people's nostalgia. W.O. Mitchell's great novel *Who has Seen the Wind?* or Mark Twain's *Huckleberry Finn* are each based on different childhoods in different landscapes. Both, however, share a depth of nostalgia with which readers instantly identify. There is something about growing up in a place that bonds us to that place. We recognize the power of that bonding experience when we find it in art and literature. We cannot help responding to the incredible emotional power of self-discovery. Nostalgia represents a gut-level, passionate reminder of those place-bonding experiences that helped to create our knowledge of ourselves: potential meeting context through time.

We know ourselves by our emerging history. I am not a name, or a biologically produced prototype of some generic species. Who else can I be, if not the sum and product of every smell I have ever smelled, every experience I have ever had, every person and place I have ever known, and every decision I have ever made? I am constantly becoming, because my environment is constantly adding to me.

If I had been conceived in a test tube and raised through parturition, weaning, walking and puberty inside a box, would I still be who I am? History has recorded cases of individuals who were cruelly deprived of context for parts of their lives. They became retarded, damaged, or incomplete. If I had been born in a different place or time, and matured in different setting or with different people, would I be the same as I am now? Clearly not.

One cannot view oneself in isolation of one's environment. Similarly, we cannot consider families, communities, nations and the human race as a whole except in the context of our collective environments. We are where we live, we are how we live, we are our environment. We are not separate; we are wholly integrated.

If a tiger in a cage is not a tiger, and a trout in a hatchery pond is no longer a trout, then are humans in an artificial social, ecological and cultural environment still human? What must we do to restore our human-ness?

Our dysfunctional western world-view has isolated

individual, community and species self-interest from the ecosystems that, ultimately, give us our context as a species. We have become so good at isolating elements from the systems they comprise that we have done the same thing to ourselves. Just as a giant liver fluke sees no need for the brain that sustains the liver, we see no need for many other organisms. Yet without the elk's brain, the liver fluke cannot exist because the elk cannot exist. Taken a step further, without elk winter range, the liver fluke cannot exist. Without forest fires that maintain that winter range, the fluke cannot be. This is a secret no liver fluke has ever suspected. Fortunately, no liver fluke has ever been able to put out fires or eradicate elk brains either.

If one cannot define the liver fluke without including those other things, neither can one identify oneself without all that connects with one. Who one is does not stop at one's skin.

A better form of anthropocentrism would, in fact, affirm that the world exists for the benefit of humankind — just as it does for tigerkind and troutkind. However, it would say that humankind, by definition, is the whole world in which it exists and which — in its well-being or its illness — shapes and creates the humans around whom existence is centred.

Anthropocentrism only becomes dysfunctional when humans choose to see themselves as separate from, and superior to, all else that exists. Anthropocentrism becomes healthy and desirable when we see ourselves as connected to, dependent upon and, ultimately, defined by all else that exists. Dysfunctional anthropocentrism makes it easy to take over a patch of scenery and wildlife habitat to build a nice country home and get the kids a horse or two. Healthful anthropocentrism would make one agonize over every decision that might reduce the natural diversity, aesthetic integrity and long-term health of the living landscape that defines one.

It makes sense to look out for your own self-interest. It

makes sense to want a better standard of living, and to protect yourself from adversity and danger. It makes sense, because every living organism does so. Through this determined self-interest organisms integrate, paradoxically, into complex, diverse, mutually sustaining ecosystems.

Humans have conscience, consciousness, intelligence, future-orientation — an entire awareness system that makes us different, we assume, from all other living creatures. This uniqueness has encouraged us to set ourselves apart from the rest of Creation. We gaze across a gulf of our own making, filled with a deep yearning for wholeness.

Those same attributes that make us unique among animals, however, can also offer a solution to the mess we have wrought of the world we love. We can draw upon them to discover that self-interest — to a species whose consciousness integrates the entirety of existence and draws upon the entirety of existence to understand itself — demands that we cherish, value, respect and nurture all of that which gives us life, meaning and identity.

I have become a passionate conservationist not because at some point in my life I entered some higher ethical plane that enabled me to place nature above self. Instead, it is because I have become gradually conscious of the fact that nature defines me. It seems obvious to me that, if I fail to act to sustain and protect the ecosystems and landscapes of my home place, then I fail to protect myself. I am the world I love. I cannot be separated from it. To damage that world, or to fail to sustain it, would be self-abuse.

This, I believe, is anthropocentrism brought back to Earth, made adaptive and honest.

Ecocentrism is not ecological. It denies the logic of self-interest by which every living thing exists. Anthropocentrism may be, in fact, as much a part of the solution as the problem.

What we need is better anthropocentrism that recognizes that — just as caged tigers and a hatchery trout are not truly tigers or trout without the living ecosystems that are their proper contexts — neither can human beings ever be truly human outside the living ecosystems that are not merely our home places, but our selves. ✽ *(1994)*

Posterity Will Bless Us

ANY GIVEN MORNING, nearly three million people wake up to the comfortable knowledge that they are Albertans. They know that there is no finer place on Earth to live out one's days than here in Alberta.

Yet each morning Alberta is a little different from what it was the yesterday. This century has seen more change than any century in the history of the planet. Change so besets Albertans that three generations of us have taken rapid, radical change for granted, as if it were the normal condition.

Where millions of grunting, constantly moving bison once washed like a living tide across miles of unfenced native prairie, now the summer sun traces rainbows across the watery veils of thousands of irrigation sprinklers watering farm fields. Where explorers struggled with deadfall and fear, asphalt highways slice mindlessly across the Rocky Mountains, past resorts and service stations. River crossing campsites have vanished under huge cities like Edmonton and Calgary. Government and industry have redefined the rivers themselves — and the soil, forests, wildlife and fishes — as resources to change, manage, and use. People are everywhere, rearranging the landscape more each day.

228

Life is too busy, most days, for most Albertans to stop and ask how much change it will take before Alberta becomes something else altogether. Few of us lose much sleep wondering what we really mean when we say that this place is Alberta, and that we are Albertans.

A province is more than its name. It is a living mosaic of human lives, landscapes, living things, and emerging history. Each of us has an image in her or his mind when we think of Alberta. The unique, natural landscapes of this part of earth are at the centre of that image. This is Wild Rose Country. Why do we say that?

How we perceive our home places, and our selves, is all tied up in the sights, smells, sounds and sensations that surround us — and become us — as our lives unfold.

Each June, for instance, I bury my face in a clump of the domestic lilacs that bloom at my mother's home in Calgary. I inhale deeply — and my brain fills instantly with a vivid image of a baby robin crouching in the corner of a rain-wet lawn. I have long ago lost the specific memory, but that image remains a part of me — a little legacy of my childhood. That baby robin is one part of that growing tapestry of experiences, memories and relationships that define this unique individual Albertan.

One spring not long ago, Gail and I floated the Milk River in southern Alberta with our small children. It had been several years since I had last been there, yet I was at home right away.

The smell of wolf willow; the wind; brown water twisting its sinuous way from cutbank to cottonwood grove to sandbar; the call of a goldfinch; thunderstorms wheeling far off across the prairie — everywhere I turned were things that were meaningful to me. I felt more myself than I had in ages. There was depth and richness not only to the landscape through which we floated, but to my response to that landscape. It was the same for Gail; she told us nostalgic anecdotes from her foothills childhood as the canyon walls slid past. Watching our kids, lost in their own present experience, I wondered what part of the Milk River Canyon was finding its way into their minds, their memories, their identities. Maybe there was a baby robin under a lilac bush there somewhere for them.

I hope so. I love those little children and I love Alberta. If there is a future for the Milk River, for the endless prairie sky, sweet winds, willets and wilderness, then there is a future worth entrusting with my children. There is a future for Alberta. Because they are all the same things, all a part of one another. They will all be the same future.

One of western society's biggest problems may be that we really do not know ourselves. Most of us are only recently come to this land that now shapes and defines us. We know our names, but not our meanings.

So, too easily, we squander the very things that are the root of our being, thinking it part of progress to write off a river here, a forest there, a wildlife population, a patch of grass-land.... We take our living heritage for granted at our own risk. In some cases, we have already lost, for all time, elements of the original Alberta. Things our grandparents knew and took for granted as characteristic of this place where they lived will never be part of how we know the same place. Like the bison and plains grizzly, they are gone. Forever.

We are our environment: the environment into which we were born, the environment that we shape and create, the environment that shapes and creates us. Why else do so many of us feel such passion for Alberta's windblown foothills, remote mountain wildnesses, far-flung northlands, rolling prairie and living rivers? It is simply because those places are who we are — because it is Alberta that makes us Albertans. In seeking to preserve some of Alberta's natural diversity, we are not promoting some abstract ideal or elitist dogma. We are seeking to defend our selves, our very identity — Creation as it is inscribed upon our souls.

This is why we need to set aside places of celebration: places that celebrate the vast variety of living systems, places and creatures that make up this province and planet. There must continue to be places to which people can return from time to time to immerse themselves in something great and humbling; to live in a basic way as citizens of the organic earth — sleeping in the sun, hunting, fishing, eating berries, drowning, fleeing from bears, or shadows; being cold, mosquito-bitten, frightened, exhilarated, exalted, enlightened and utterly humbled. There must always be places where people can take their children to learn what it is to be of this place: to be woven into a work of art so immense, complex and intricately detailed that we can never hope to comprehend the Art, let alone the Artist.

Who we are today is the product of the rich natural diversity Albertans have been blessed to inherit. Who we will become tomorrow depends, to a large degree, on what we save of wild Alberta today.

A vision of an Alberta that preserves all of its original beauty and natural diversity led to the Endangered Spaces campaign, one that unites Alberta conservationists from every walk of life. The government of Alberta now has a plan, too, which promises to protect a small portion of natural Alberta. Which vision prevails — if either — will depend upon what Albertans demand of their political representatives.

When ranchers near Pincher Creek persuaded Canada's Minister of the Interior in 1895 to set aside Waterton Lakes National Park as a legacy for future generations, he wrote: "Posterity will bless us." He was right.

It could bless us too. ❧ *(1993)*

Recognition

I SET MY CANOE INTO THE SILT-GREY waters of the Athabasca River one evening and slipped quietly away into the gloom.

It was barely May, too early in the year for birdsong. The only sounds were the muted chuckle of the river and the occasional distant hiss and whine of passing traffic on the Yellowhead Highway. Elk watched my canoe drift past. Higher, on the open slopes of Mount Colin, a herd of bighorn sheep picked their way up a shadowed meadow. They knew where they were going. I did not.

They were at home. I was just passing by.

I had thought about doing my field work on foot with a flashlight, but commonsense suggested I look for alternatives. Grizzlies haunt the river flats in early spring, avoiding the lingering snowpack of the high country while they forage on sweet vetch roots and winterkill. The thought of meeting a grizzly nose-to-nose in the dark was sufficient to make me look for other ways of counting owls.

Owls were only a few of about 250 species of vertebrate animals I was supposed to inventory for Parks Canada. Soil scientists and botanists had already mapped this part of Jasper, tracing lines around discrete ecosystems and landforms. Now it was my turn to document how many mammals, birds, reptiles and amphibians were at home in each ecosite, as we called the map units.

Owls are hard to find except in early spring when they give their distinctive territorial calls. I had no choice but to seek them at night, which is why I was now tunnelling silently into the gloom. My canoe tipped and tilted beneath me, responding to the icy boils and back eddies of a river that, a few miles upstream, was glacier ice. I looked into the silt-shadowed water

and shivered, contemplating the consequences of an unexpected encounter with a sweeper.

A boreal owl tootled briefly as I slipped past a large
stand of old-growth white spruce. From time to time I heard
the familiar hooting of a great horned owl or the monotonous
high-pitched whistles of a saw-whet. Once something went
crashing out of shallow water and vanished into forest gloom.

The moon rose beyond Roche Miette. It silvered the
landscape, casting trees into relief and spilling a path of silver
across the river's rippled surface. Navigating was easier now.
The lower Athabasca River in Jasper National Park is fast-flow-
ing but gentle. I was not too worried about swamping. Still, it
was good to be able to watch out for sweepers or gravel bars in
the cold glow of the moon.

The mountains silhouetted on either side stretched off
to the northwest and the southeast, separated by high valleys
trending in the same direction. I had seen these mountains
once out the window of a commercial jet. From that elevation
they looked like giant waves that had suddenly hardened in
place — long lines of limestone breakers forever waiting to
crash down on west-central Alberta's boreal plains.

From canoe-level I could see the way in which each
range ended abruptly at the edge of the Athabasca River.
Glaciers long ago shaved off and steepened the mountain ends.
A few thousand years ago the glaciers melted back to where
they wait, now, cupped among the highest peaks, poised to
advance down-valley again when the climate cools again.

Those shrunken glaciers fed the river on which I now
floated. The valley's glacial origin was obvious to me; even the
mighty Athabasca River is too small to have carved the broad
valley through which it flows. It was a river of ice, not water,
that carved this valley.

Another owl tootled, high on the forested benchlands

233

above the river. I back paddled, ferrying away from a spruce sweeper and bouncing down a shallow riffle. A pair of geese began to clamour. Their long necks bobbed up and down as they paced me down the far side of a midstream island. They were still complaining when the canoe carried me around a bend.

A sudden confusion of channels glistened in the moonlight. The river widened here, slowing as it approached Jasper Lake.

A freshening breeze — spilling down the broad valley from the high country to the west — nudged the canoe gently out of the main channel. I had to paddle hard to get back into the current. The channel turned. The breeze pushed me toward the bank.

The channels widened and coalesced as the current bore me out onto the shallow waters of Jasper Lake. Twice I ran aground on silt, pushed off, drifted a few yards, and ran aground again. The water was wave-rippled, silt-laden and secret. It offered no clues where the deep channel had gone.

Jasper Lake is only a lake for part of each year. When the glaciers melted back, they left the valleys of the Athabasca and its tributaries filled with loose gravel, silt, clay and other debris. The Snake Indian River joins the Athabasca from the northwest at the same point where the Rocky River enters from the southeast. Both rivers swept countless tons of raw sediment out of their new valleys each year for centuries, depositing it where they lost power upon entering the main Athabasca valley. Over the years, both rivers built alluvial fans that spread across the valley and joined, blocking the Athabasca and damming up Jasper Lake.

The Athabasca also carries a heavy load of sediment. Pooled behind the natural dam, the Athabasca has deposited ten-centuries-worth of silt and sand in Jasper Lake. What began as a lake is now a deep deposit of fine glacial flour. Only in summer, when the Columbia Icefield and other headwater glaciers melt most feverishly, does water cover the silt flats and Jasper Lake again become worthy of the name.

Tonight was a bad night to paddle Jasper Lake. The spring runoff had begun to cover the silt flats but the resulting lake was only a few inches deep at best. Bit by bit, by trial and error, I found the deep-water channel, drifted further into the lake, and ran aground again. Even when I was sure of where the channel lay, the stiffening breeze confounded me by blowing the canoe off course. Repeatedly I found the channel, only to lose it and run aground.

Finally, in frustration, I decided to wade across the moonlit lake to shore, cache my canoe beside the highway, and hitchhike home. I stepped out of the canoe, grabbed the bow rope, and began to walk. Semi-trailer truck rigs burrowed through the darkness along the south edge of the lake. I was just contemplating the shock that one of those truck drivers would experience if he or she happened to look my way and see a man walking across the surface of a lake, pulling a canoe, when I had a shock of my own: I found the missing channel.

Soaked, furious and frustrated, I gripped the side of the canoe and drifted until my feet found the silty bottom again. I clambered back into the canoe and began to paddle down the channel. The wind took control and again blew me aground in shallow water.

Exasperated and discouraged, I sat shivering in the darkness, watching wind ripples chasing down the long silver reflection of the moon. Listening to the stillness, I became aware of a strange, high-pitched hiss like vibrating power lines. There were no power lines, however. Alone in mid-lake, I listened carefully. The sound seemed to come from the canoe.

Leaning over, I watched the grip and scurry of water

flowing along the sides of the canoe. All at once it dawned on me that what I was hearing was the saltating hiss of millions of tiny silt particles. Silt was sliding against the aluminum as the river bore it out into the lake. Glaciers had ground this flour-like silt from mountain rock. The melted waters of those same glaciers carried it in suspension down-valley to my canoe, and Jasper Lake.

As I contemplated my discovery, a low moan rose out of the darkness far across the lake, swelling into a long, resonating howl. It faded, died, and was gone, leaving only a faint hissing, the tug of wind on wet clothing, and a silver line of moonlight spilling across a dark lake.

Later that night I finally made it to shore, stashed my canoe, and went home to a hot bath and a dry bed. When I awoke the next day, the Athabasca valley was transformed.

I had thought I knew the Athabasca River: its valley-bottom forests, steep-walled mountains and wolves. I had visited the headwater glaciers. I understood the story of how they had once extended east onto the central Alberta plains. But that night in the middle of Jasper Lake was the first time I came to see that they were not separate things: all were one.

The wind that blew my canoe aground had only recent-ly kissed the surface of glaciers that were the source of the water on which I floated. The same west wind, year after year, had pulled moisture in off the Pacific Ocean, lifted it high into the Rockies, and shed it as snow — the snow that fed those glaciers.

Depleted of moisture, warmed by the sudden descent to low elevations, those same winds funnelled down the Athabasca valley — which those same glaciers had carved in times gone by — and swept winter snows away. In doing so, the west wind helped create a rich habitat mosaic for elk, sheep, deer and other animals upon which the wolf I had heard relied for food.

Silt ground by glacier ice from those high mountains,

washed downstream by glacier meltwater, had filled Jasper Lake. Each winter, when the glaciers froze rock-hard, the lake level fell. Those same west winds swept up the silt, depositing it in dunes where those same wolves denned.

Wind and ice, river and mountain, wolf and water: all were part of the same whole. All were linked by cause and effect, time and consequence. All were threads in the same landscape tapestry.

For days I gazed around me, wide-eyed, seeing my home landscape as if for the first time. My midnight awakening had opened me to discovery. Over the months and years that followed, my intimacy with this place deepened and accreted as I followed the threads of my discovery into new understandings.

Years earlier, a friend had a similar experience. Dale Zieroth and I worked as park naturalists in Kootenay National Park. He was a poet by choice and a historian by training. Each summer Dale chose a subject about which he knew little, and forced himself to learn all he could about that it. Then he sought within his imagination a way to bring it to life in the interpretive programs he delivered in campground theatres.

One year he decided to focus on glacial geomorphology — how glaciers change landscapes. He knew next to nothing about it. Every day he cloistered himself in the park library, poring over geography books. He poured himself into a crash course on aretes, eskers, moraines, hanging valleys and all the various landscape features that result when ice, rock and water spend a long time in each other's company. Each evening he drove home, bemused, from the park office in Radium Hot Springs to his house on a hillside near Invermere.

By mid-May he was irritable and distracted. He had filled himself with facts, but nothing had gelled. He knew the details, but he could not find a story.

Then one day he flew into the office, ecstatic.

"What happened?" I asked.

"I've got it!"

"What?"

"An esker connection," he cried, grinning with relief. "I've made an esker connection."

The previous evening, driving down highway 93 in the golden light of a May evening, Dale had found himself slowing as usual where the pavement traced an elegant S-bend along the benches above Stoddart Creek.

"All at once," he said, "I realized that the S-bend was there because they built the highway right along the top of an esker. I've driven that S-bend almost every day for years. I'd never even wondered about it before. And then I looked around and I saw that the benches were kame terraces. Then I saw other eskers and drumlins in the valley bottom, and hanging valleys along the edge of the Columbia valley...."

Deer were feeding on the sunburnt side of a kame terrace. A raven drifted above the esker, looking for road kills. Dale came home that night through a landscape he had never seen before. The irony confounded him: he and his wife had built a house, raised a child and spent years delighting in the surroundings they had chosen for home. Yet they had never seen the eskers.

Most animals are acutely aware of landscape. Humans, for the most part, can choose to ignore it.

We do not need to seek out sunbathed south-facing slopes on cold days in fall; we merely turn up the thermostat. We do not retreat to the shelter of old-growth forests or seek a familiar rock overhang when the rain falls; we go indoors. Engineers design our roads for speed so that we can waste as little time as possible when we travel between artificial places of our own creation. Highways negate landscape. The engineers who build them fill valleys and carve down hills so that drivers need not notice the natural ups and downs. All the curves are smooth. Mileage signs tell us how much longer until we escape the landscape and get home.

Ranchers, loggers and others who make their living outdoors are necessarily more aware of landscape than most of those who huddle in cities and towns. Hunters — true hunters who leave their vehicles behind and venture quietly into the wild — seek to become creatures of landscape much in the same way as their prey.

All, however, return at night to heated homes, flick on the lights, settle before the television, eat something from the fridge. All are part of a culture that assumes going home must entail turning one's back on the living landscape.

There used to be people who viewed things differently. Keith Brady, a park warden, showed me one of their camps in Waterton Lakes National Park one day. It was at a place called Indian Springs.

The campsite filled a grassy bay where rolling fescue grassland swept up against an aspen-covered sidehill. A small spring issued from the ground and chuckled away into the prairie.

"That spring doesn't freeze in winter," Keith said. "They would have had water all year round."

A nearby ridge gave the people who dwelt here shelter from wind, too. Trees grew tall along the ridge and around a nearby wetland. Shelter from wind, in a landscape where winter winds commonly gust to hurricane intensity and last for days on end, is a vital matter to every living creature.

Firewood was abundant on the hill above. The long-gone people whose campsite we had found would only have had to drag it downhill.

We sat our horses, studying the landscape. Chief

Mountain, one of the most important mountains in the Blackfoot Nation's mythology, stood forth from the rest of the Rockies several miles to the east. Closer, a complex of eskers, moraines and hollows stretched along the edge of the Waterton River valley. Wind-whipped grassland covered the knolls and ridges. A few bison fed on the crest of one hillock. They were part of a captive herd; a century ago there would have been wild bison in the same place. The Waterton valley's howling winds ensure that this eskerine complex remains snow-free — except lee slopes and hollows — through most winters.

The native hunters who camped at Indian Springs hunted the bison by herding them down the long draws between eskers and forcing them into deep snowdrifts where they could slaughter the big animals. The people camped at the one place in the landscape where they were consistently assured of open water, shelter, firewood, and proximity to good hunting. There was no need to go home after hunting. They were already there — like the bison, the aspens, the wind and the eskers.

Modern North America's landscapes are now our homes too. We just tend not to think of them that way. Instead we drift, unanchored, into a future that frightens most of us, feeling vaguely incomplete, but unable to define that which is missing. We profess concern about "the environment," but it is an objectively defined environment — not a subjective home — about which we express an abstract concern. Our concern, in any case, is limited to those brief periods when other matters, concerning the world-within-a-world we have created, do not distract us.

We can always "go home" and shut the door when it all gets too much for us.

Gail and I lived briefly in a bedroom community south of Calgary. We chose Okotoks because the Calgary we had both grown up in was long gone. We hoped a small foothills town might offer some kind of link to the things of the past we value

240

most. Reality soon disillusioned us.

All that first summer I watched over the back fence as a developer eradicated one square mile of foothills landscape. As the summer progressed, heavy equipment rebuilt it into a generic suburb that might have been anywhere in the western world: a placeless colony for domesticated humans. The northwest-southeast glacial scours vanished; branching, interlinked roadways replaced them. Bulldozers and earth-movers recontoured and dammed the coulee to make little ponds and terraces. The swales that once spilled spring runoff into the coulee vanished overnight. The new landscape had a new hydrology, buried in sewer pipes. Exotic shrubs and lawns of tame bluegrass replaced the native fescue, wheatgrass, silverberry and pasture sage. The very scent of the place changed: silver willow musk, wild rose and curing hay gave way to 2-4,D, dust and engine exhaust.

By the time the first snow fell, another piece of Alberta landscape had become mere real estate. Looking around at the street where we lived, I realized that only a decade or so ago it, too, had been foothills prairie. Yet Gail and I, our neighbours, and those hopeful young families moving into the new subdivision next door, proudly declared ourselves Albertans. We professed to be at home here, amid all the For Sale signs.

By the time we left, Okotoks had become a place of horrified realization: the flip side of Dale's esker connection. It had forced me to see, beneath the common and accepted urban cityscapes and pastoral farmscapes among which I grew up, the fading shadows of what could, and should, have been home. I felt as if I had watched helplessly as vandals defaced my home — and then, as one turned, seen that he wore my face.

When we moved to Okotoks Gail and I were closer than we had been in years to the houses where we grew up and the places we had known in youth. We soon realized we were more homesick than we had ever been. We had tried to go

241

home. We just had not known what that meant.

We moved again, coming home to Waterton, far from the scrapers, cats and landscaping companies. Still, they are not far behind. The dust cloud of haste and unconcern will continue to rise from the near horizon until we western Canadians succeed in redefining home and establishing a more reflective and honourable relationship with the places of which fate grants us the chance to be a part. Like the vandals in my vision, those scrapers, cats and contractors wear our faces. Our eyes stare blankly from those faces, failing to focus as they sweep the living landscape. Interest flickers only when they see familiar things — bank machines, televisions, asphalt, other products of artifice and desire.

What we recognize depends upon what we can see. What we see depends upon how our senses have been trained: who we are. Who we are depends, usually, on the kind of home we grew up in.

I still return to my family home at Christmas and Thanksgiving. I visit my mother in the house that has been a part of my life since the age of four. There is a crucifix on the dining room wall; I remember holy cards tucked behind it after my first Communion and palm leaves drying behind it each spring. I know which stairs squeak, what the furnace sounds like late at night, which walls are patched, and why. Everything about that house is familiar, rich with association, memory and significance. The faces around the table are people I know and love. We have laughed together, suffered together, learned to give each other space and to take pleasure in the times when we reunite.

That house and those people are home. They matter deeply to me. I could not stand to be cut off from them. I could never bring myself to do harm to any of them. They are all inextricably bound up in how I have come to know my self.

So, too, I now know, are the Athabasca River valley, the eskers and kames south of Radium, the wind-whipped aspen forests of Waterton, and the wild places and living landscapes I've come to know — however imperfectly — and grown to love through years of exploration, contemplation and growing concern about their well-being.

It is time to come home. It is past time. It is time for each of us to rediscover the living landscapes of the wounded West and recognize them as the home places that make us who we are — no less than our families, the houses in which we live and the ways in which we earn our livings. It is time to seek our own esker connections — moments of epiphany that transfigure our surroundings and transform us. No matter how hard we race toward the horizon, it recedes ahead of us. Perhaps home is not beyond the horizon after all. Coming home may be a simple matter of learning to see more clearly where we are already. ❧

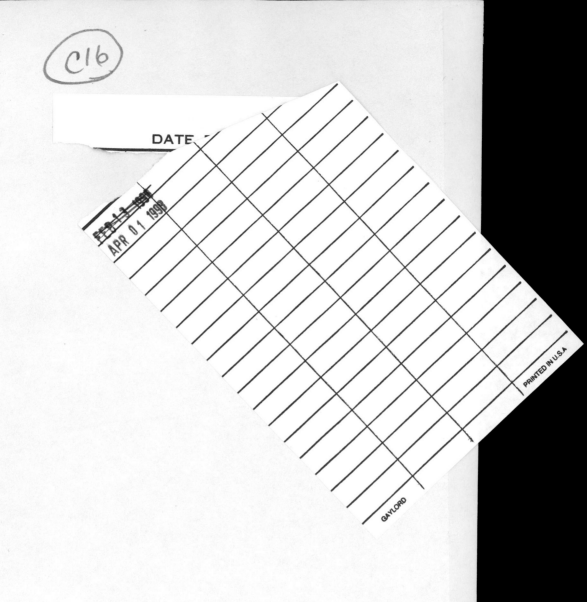